Editor-in-Chief and Founder:
  Lyndon H. LaRouche, Jr.
Editorial Board: *Lyndon H. LaRouche, Jr. , Helga
  Zepp-LaRouche, Paul Gallagher, Tony Papert,
  Gerald Rose, Dennis Small, Jeffrey Steinberg,
  William Wertz*
Co-Editors: *Paul Gallagher, Tony Papert*
Managing Editor: *Nancy Spannaus*
Technology: *Marsha Freeman*
Books: *Katherine Notley*
Ebooks: *Richard Burden*
Graphics: *Alan Yue*
Photos: *Stuart Lewis*
Circulation Manager: *Stanley Ezrol*

INTELLIGENCE DIRECTORS
Counterintelligence: *Jeffrey Steinberg, Michele
  Steinberg*
Economics: *John Hoefle, Marcia Merry Baker,
  Paul Gallagher*
History: *Anton Chaitkin*
Ibero-America: *Dennis Small*
Russia and Eastern Europe: *Rachel Douglas*
United States: *Debra Freeman*

INTERNATIONAL BUREAUS
Bogotá: *Miriam Redondo*
Berlin: *Rainer Apel*
Copenhagen: *Tom Gillesberg*
Houston: *Harley Schlanger*
Lima: *Sara Madueño*
Melbourne: *Robert Barwick*
Mexico City: *Gerardo Castilleja Chávez*
New Delhi: *Ramtanu Maitra*
Paris: *Christine Bierre*
Stockholm: *Ulf Sandmark*
United Nations, N.Y.C.: *Leni Rubinstein*
Washington, D.C.: *William Jones*
Wiesbaden: *Göran Haglund*

ON THE WEB
e-mail: eirns@larouchepub.com
www.larouchepub.com
www.executiveintelligencereview.com
www.larouchepub.com/eiw
Webmaster: *John Sigerson*
Assistant Webmaster: *George Hollis*
Editor, Arabic-language edition: *Hussein Askary*

EIR (ISSN 0273-6314) *is published weekly
(50 issues), by EIR News Service, Inc.,
P.O. Box 17390, Washington, D.C. 20041-0390.
(703) 777-9451*

European Headquarters: E.I.R. GmbH, Postfach
Bahnstrasse 9a, D-65205, Wiesbaden, Germany
Tel: 49-611-73650
Homepage: http://www.eirna.com
e-mail: eirna@eirna.com
Director: Georg Neudecker

Montreal, Canada: 514-461-1557

Denmark: EIR - Danmark, Sankt Knuds Vej 11,
basement left, DK-1903 Frederiksberg, Denmark.
Tel.: +45 35 43 60 40, Fax: +45 35 43 87 57. e-mail:
eirdk@hotmail.com.

Mexico City: EIR, Sor Juana Inés de la Cruz 242-2
Col. Agricultura C.P. 11360
Delegación M. Hidalgo, México D.F.
Tel. (5525) 5318-2301
eirmexico@gmail.com

Canada Post Publication Sales Agreement
#40683579

Postmaster: Send all address changes to *EIR*, P.O.
Box 17390, Washington, D.C. 20041-0390.

Signed articles in *EIR* represent the views of the
authors, and not necessarily those of the Editorial
Board.

Galactic Man

EIR Contents

www.larouchepub.com   Volume 42, Number 20, May 15, 2015

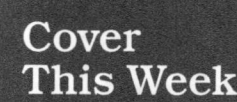

Cover This Week

"The Giant" by Francisco Goya

Harris Brisbane Dick Fund, 1935

Galactic Man: Shadow versus Principle

The following is a transcript of the May 6, 2015 New Paradigm for Mankind show (https://larouchepac.com/new-paradigm), featuring Megan Beets, Ben Deniston, and Liona Fan-Chiang of the LaRouchePAC Science Team.

Megan Beets: The topic of our discussion today is the responsibility for defining a clear conceptual direction for the mission of mankind. And that's not something that 99% of the population even comes close to thinking about, or believe that they should be thinking about. But that's human. That's a human responsibility. That's the responsibility of a kind of creature, a kind of species, which is an immortal species, which has the possibility to contribute something and define something after their mortal life is over.

So that's what we're here to discuss today. What are the true principles, what are the true controlling universal principles, which define our actions here on Earth, and will define new, and open up new, possibilities for action, perhaps beyond the Earth? And that's why Lyndon LaRouche has put so much emphasis on the recent work that you've been doing, Ben, on the water cycle, and locating the terrestrial water cycle within a larger system which is governed by a principle which we have yet to completely master and discover, which is this galactic principle. So I'll let you elaborate.

We Live in a Galactic System

Ben Deniston: I thought today it would be good to go through a bit of an elaboration of this. For maybe a little more than a month now, we've been developing this renewed focus on the role of the galaxy in shaping the water cycle, climate, weather on Earth, especially in the context of the drought in California, and the growing water crisis. We've put a lot on the table in the last month. I thought, given the work we've done, it would be a good opportunity to go through, and add some more depth to various aspects.

What I'm going to go through is broken up into three parts. I have a lot of graphics and visuals to go

Ben Deniston

through this. We really want to continue to develop this as a coherent picture. We've started to develop, and Mr. LaRouche has picked up on, a revolution, an understanding in a completely new way, that we exist not just on Earth, obviously—people have known that. We live in the Solar System. You can't isolate Earth from the Solar System. Kepler showed us that. It's not new.

We've known that we live in a galactic system, but the way that's been treated and understood, is that there's this vague, big, empty space out there that we're kind of in the middle of, that has no real relation, or influence, on what we do here on Earth. It's kind of "out there," outside. Maybe some academic people will talk about it, but when it comes to day-to-day activity, people don't think about the fact we're living in a galaxy.

Well, what we're seeing now, with this water crisis, is the failure to approach it from a competent standpoint—we have to understand this. And the failure right now to understand these processes on Earth, including the water cycle, as being driven by these higher processes—it is mankind's challenge now, today, at this point in history, to begin to tackle that, and understand that.

With that new capability, as I want to really develop here today: We're talking about a completely new relationship that mankind can have to the system. We're not talking about just how to get a little bit of water. This is not some small thing, where we can just kind of quickly get a little bit of water here, and help out a little bit. We're talking about opening up a whole new potential where mankind can manage the system in a completely new way, from a completely new standpoint.

And it is this galactic standpoint: from the standpoint of the principle of the galaxy, as a subsuming system, which encompasses and defines the Solar System as a subsumed process, and then the Earth therein, as a subsumed process. That it's really mankind making a certain creative leap, understanding the role of the galaxy, which enables us to then act differently, to have new powers here on Earth, and then to solve all these problems.

So, I want to go through three phases of developing this for people, so we can have a solid presentation of what we have so far, as the picture of this new galactic frontier. We're in the galactic frontier; we just have to *realize* we're in the galactic frontier.

To start, picking up from some of what we discussed on the Friday webcast, I think it's by emphasizing the concept of shadow versus principle. People see weather phenomena, people see aspects of the water cycle. You see clouds, you see evidence for how water behaves in the atmosphere. You experience rainfall. You experience these things.

But these are really shadows. They're things created. They're not self-determined. They don't create themselves. We depend upon their effects, and we depend upon our ability to manage their effects. That's what's enabled us to grow and develop as a species. But they are effects. They're shadows of something.

Up until this point, it has been assumed, largely, that you're just talking about an Earth-Sun interaction. The Sun evaporates water; it heats the atmosphere. It provides atmospheric water vapor by evaporating from the oceans. And then various processes on Earth are involved in how that water behaves, and how it moves through this cyclical system.

Until recently, aside from the work of a relative handful of scientists, that's been it. It's an Earth-Sun system. Those are the factors at play. There's nothing else going on. That's what defines the system. You have a lot of variations. You have the role of the oceans on Earth; you have the role of life on Earth, but these are all sort of subsets, or components, of this Solar System process. This interaction of what the Sun's doing and what the Earth's doing, which creates these shadows, these effects. They determine what the water cycle does, how the water cycle behaves.

But, what we see is that we have deviations in these shadows. These shadows behave differently than we would expect, by this prior hypothesis. We see variations in how these shadows behave, how the water cycle expresses itself, which we cannot attribute to just this current conception of how the Sun and the Earth interact.

Outside the Solar System

Just to really make this clear, I have a series of studies here that I want to go through. The first sequence here, is just to illustrate how we see this deviation, this variation, in the activity of the water cycle, of these shadows, across all time-scales: in the course of short time-scales—years, decades; on the scale of centuries; on the scale of thousands of years; on the scale of millions and hundreds of millions of years. Over this huge, vast sweep of different time-scales, we see variations which we cannot attribute to the current understanding of the activity of a Sun-Earth interaction, but point us instead to the galaxy, to the galactic system, to

FIGURE 1

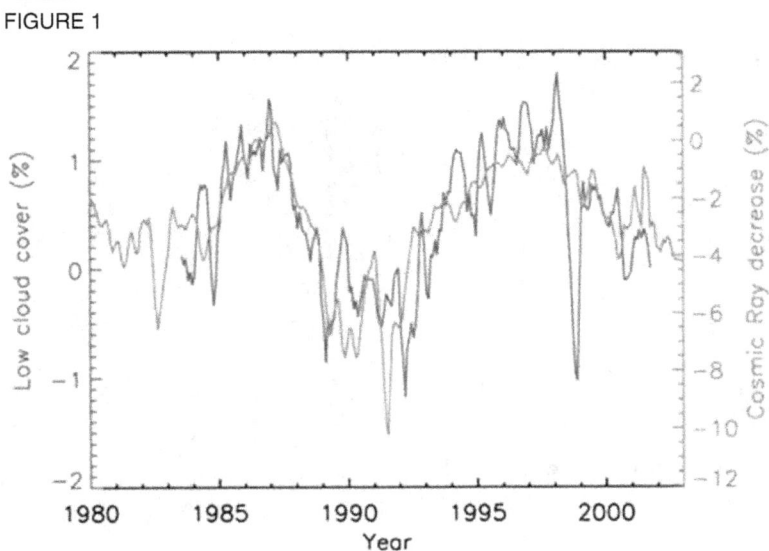

the input from the galactic environment creating the conditions which control these shadows, control these effects.

So, I have a series of graphs from studies which show this across these successive time-scales. We're going to take our minds back in increasing lengths of periods of time, to show that we keep seeing these variations, pointing to this other principle, this other factor, outside of the Solar System itself.

Figure 1: This is a graphic showing the relation between galactic radiation, radiation coming in from the galaxy, as the effect of the galactic system impinging on our atmosphere, affecting Earth's environment, showing the variation of that, with the variation of low-level cloud cover.

This is something that really stirred a lot of excitement when it was published, led by the work of Henrik Svensmark, a Danish professor, and some of his associates. It showed that variations in the flux of galactic cosmic radiation, activity from the galaxy, directly relates to variations in low-level cloud formation and cloud cover.

This, in particular, is also related to variations in solar activity, because the Sun plays a major role by its magnetic influence, in shielding the Solar System from this galactic influence. So, think of the Sun as creating a force field, a magnetic environment, around the Solar System; and as the Sun strengthens or weakens, that force field, that surrounding magnetic field, changes how much influence we get from the galaxy. So this is the Sun playing a certain role in modulating the amount of this galactic influence on the system.

Now, again, by the prior conception, the role of this magnetic activity of the Sun should have no effect on how the water cycle behaves, how the climate works, how weather behaves. They limit it just to the heating effect of the Sun, the direct sunlight; that's supposed to be the only influence the Sun has on the Earth's water system, the climate, etc. The magnetic field shouldn't have an influence, according to the prior conception.

But we see that the magnetic field *does* have an influence in modulating how much of this galactic effect comes in.

So, this created a big stir. It got a lot of the people who are part of the Church of the IPCC [Intergovernmental Panel on Climate Change] really freaked out, these religious adherents to the doctrine of Prince Philip and his like, that mankind is having catastrophic, devastating effects on the climate by driving cars, and trying to provide electricity for people. That whole insane, genocidal framework was rather worried when it came out that we're seeing the evidence that major variations in climate are not attributed just to man's activity, but to the activity of this cosmic process, this cosmic input.

People probably know something about this, probably heard something about this role of cosmic rays, galactic cosmic radiation, in affecting cloud formation.

Beets: And these low-level clouds have an effect on global temperature, right?

Deniston: Right. They showed that a very small—a couple percentage points—change in the amount of low-level cloud cover, can have a huge effect on the global temperature. So the crazy Church of the IPCC goes into these crazy twists and turns, to try and amplify the effects of CO_2, to try to come up with some scheme to claim that the increase of this tiny trace gas in the atmosphere is having catastrophic effects.

Meanwhile, a tiny variation in cloud cover plays a huge role in controlling how much sunlight comes into the Earth.

The Sun's Magnetic Activity

Beets: And the magnetic activity of the Sun varies a lot more than its light.

Deniston: Yes. According to our current ideas, the amount of sunlight, technically, the electro-magnetic radiation, the radiation that comes at the speed of light—infrared, visible light—the total amount of energy

FIGURE 2

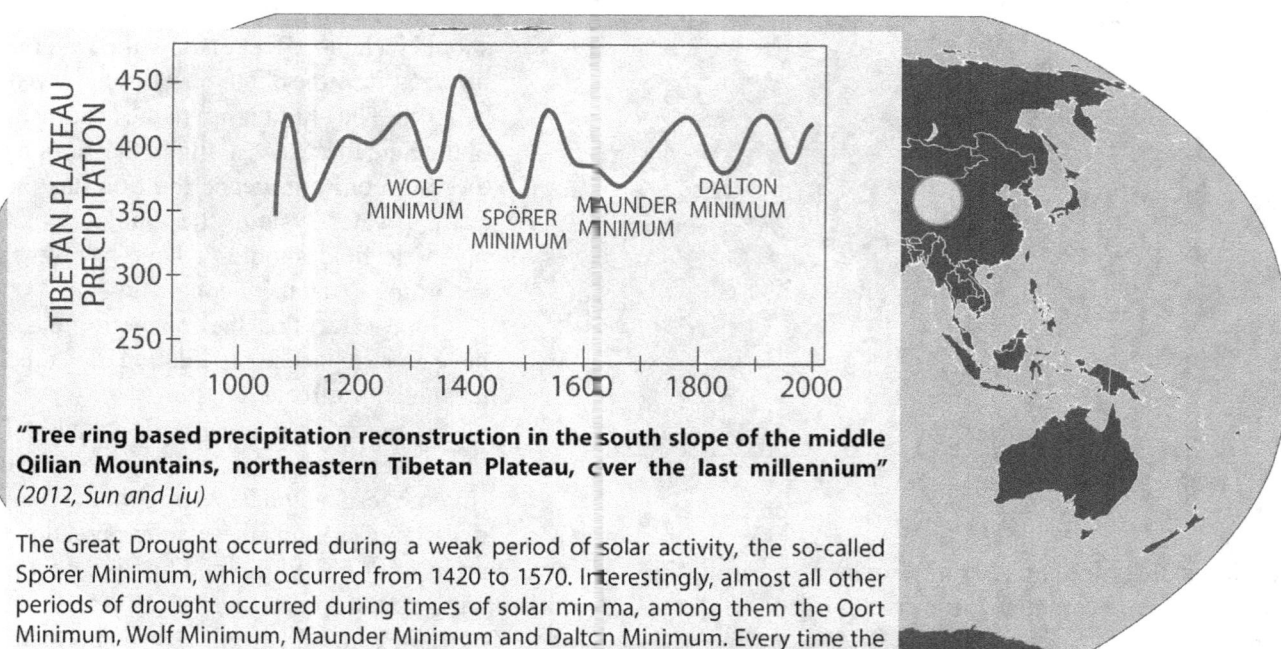

"Tree ring based precipitation reconstruction in the south slope of the middle Qilian Mountains, northeastern Tibetan Plateau, over the last millennium" (2012, Sun and Liu)

The Great Drought occurred during a weak period of solar activity, the so-called Spörer Minimum, which occurred from 1420 to 1570. Interestingly, almost all other periods of drought occurred during times of solar minima, among them the Oort Minimum, Wolf Minimum, Maunder Minimum and Dalton Minimum. Every time the sun goes into a slumber for a few decades, the rains on the Tibetan Plateau stay away.

coming from that, doesn't seem to vary too much. But the magnetic field goes through wild fluctuations.

It's pretty incredible that the Sun's magnetic field reverses about every decade. You think of the size of the Sun. If you've seen the Sun compared to the Earth in scale, you're thinking of a system that big, on not a geological time-scale, but on a human time-scale. In ten, eleven, twelve years the Sun goes through a complete pole reversal in its magnetic field. It's really a remarkable process going on.

So the Sun—you look at it in the sky, it doesn't look as if it's doing too much. It's doing the same thing today that it was doing yesterday. But if you look at it with the increasing sophistication of our new instruments, to measure its magnetic effect, to measure its atmosphere, and various other conditions created by solar activity, you see it's going through wild variations. It's a pretty active player.

But our interest here is in the fact that it plays kind of a gatekeeper role in modulating the galactic influence, which is what we're most interested in, and we'll get into in the second and third parts of this discussion. This galactic influence is the critical factor that's giving us new insight into what the system is, but then also, a new potential to manage that system, from this galactic insight, from the insight into the principle of the galactic system.

Anyway, to set that up, we have these things. These are deviations. These are anomalies. What you're looking at here is an anomaly relative to the current understanding. There shouldn't be a relationship, under the current mainstream framework, between cosmic ray flux, and cloud cover. And because of the danger this poses to the man-made global warming scare, you see people going nuts, and trying to attack this thing, but, we see the effects.

So this is an anomaly, and this is one, again, that stirred up a lot of commotion over the past couple of decades now—that people can demonstrate this effect.

I want to take this as a starting point. This is from 1980 to 2003-04—this is a couple decades of activity, where we see the behavior of clouds, which are part of the water cycle in the atmosphere—the behavior of clouds varying with these variations in the galactic influence, the amount of influence we get from our galactic system.

Broader Time-Scales

Let's take this to broader time-scales, one or two examples from a succession of time-scales, where you see a consistent expression of these deviations, these so-called anomalies, from the earlier framework.

Figure 2: This is one that I've identified a couple times on these shows. It's one of a number of studies that show precipitation, also climate and temperature, varying in direct correspondence with the amount of galactic influence, which, again, is associated with how active the Sun is.

But here we're not talking about the last two and a half decades. We're talking about the last 1,000 years. So, we looked at one small time-scale, decades; now we're looking at 1,000 years, a larger time-scale, within which we would still expect these decadal variations to occur. But on top of that, we now see evidence of large variations, within which the smaller variations are nested.

So, we see over the past 10 centuries, the past 1,000 years, here in particular, variations in precipitation, the amount of rainfall on the Tibet Plateau in China, corresponding directly with periods when you get very low solar activity, and high galactic influence. And when you get this high galactic influence, in this particular region, you get lower precipitation; you get drought. And you see that consistently across these minimums, these periods when the Sun got really weak, that allowed the galaxy to have a stronger role in the system. And, corresponding with that, we see variations in rainfall, precipitation, and periods of drought corresponding to this increased galactic influence.

Again, let's take a kind of trip across these time-scales. We see the decadal variation; now we see variations corresponding to the time-scales of centuries.

We can keep going farther. **Figure 3:** This is a depiction of the variation in the galactic, cosmic radiation, and the variation in rainfall, measured in Oman on the Arabian Peninsula, from a period of about 7,900 years ago, to about a little over 8,300 years ago. So again, going back ten to twelve thousands of years, you still see there's a very close, direct relationship between variations in the amount of galactic influence, and how these shadows of the water cycle, precipitation, occur on Earth.

This is a total anomaly from the standpoint of the prior framework.

Take another step back. This is

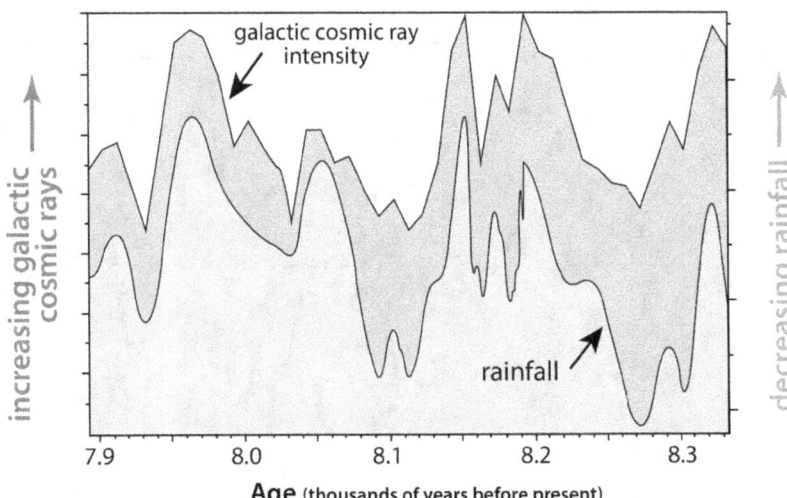

FIGURE 3

GALACTIC COSMIC RAYS AND RAINFALL

increasing galactic cosmic rays →

decreasing rainfall →

galactic cosmic ray intensity

rainfall

Age (thousands of years before present)

7.9   8.0   8.1   8.2   8.3

source: Jasper Kirkby, 2008

now looking at the whole timespan of the last 12,000 years (**Figure 4**). So again, decadal time-scales, time-scales of hundreds of years, and now we're looking at thousands of years.

Now again, we see indications—we have measurements of the amount of galactic influence, the galactic cosmic radiation flux, here in the purplish color. And very tightly associated with that, we see variations in the glaciation effects, the amount of ice flow, and the movement of ice in the North Atlantic.

In particular, this is measuring the amount of debris and stuff brought down into the oceans by ice. As ice moves across the land, into the oceans, it deposits the dirt

FIGURE 4

ICE RAFTED DEBRIS VS COSMIC RAYS (MEASURED BY ^{14}C)
Thousands of Years

ICE RAFTED DEBRIS

^{14}C

12,000 YEARS AGO   6,000 YEARS AGO   NOW

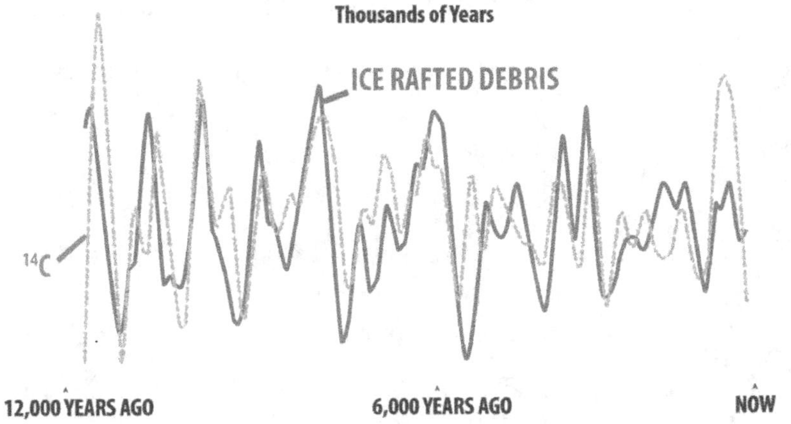

source: Jasper Kirkby, 2008

FIGURE 5

GALACTIC COSMIC RAY FLUX AND TEMPERATURE

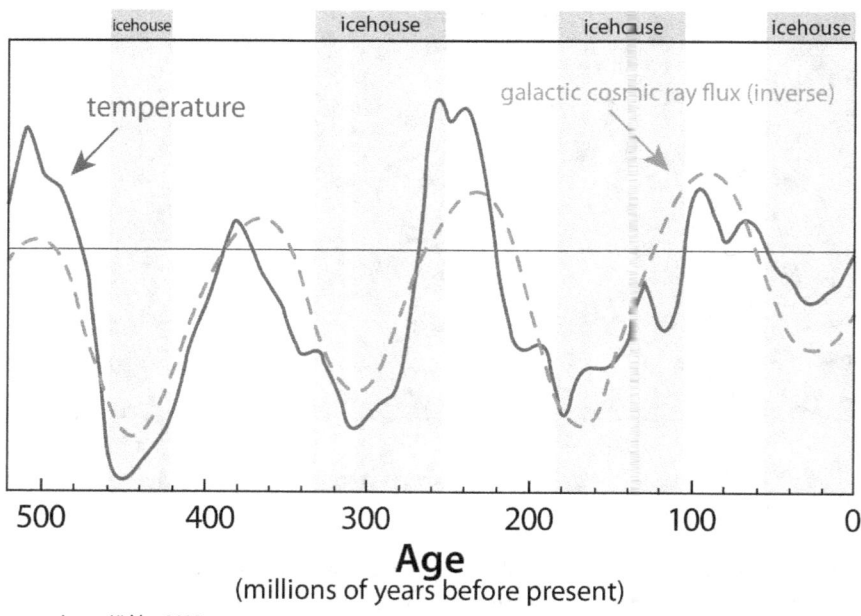

source: Jasper Kirkby, 2008

hundreds of millions of years. We again see variations in the climate, climate records, associated with changes in the galactic environment.

Figure 5: This is one we've discussed a number of times, where we have indications according to our current ideas of how the Solar System moves through the galaxy. When we move through the spiral arms, experience different environments, we see changes in the climate system. In particular, very large glaciation, major global cooling events, associated with regions of more active galactic activity. Associated with the spiral arms, for example, in this study.

You also see variations in the climate, the temperature, corresponding to the motion of our Solar System, above and below the galactic plane (**Figure 6**).

and the rocks and the stones that it brings. We're looking at different proxy records, and shadows, that indicate these variations in the climate, and the environment.

So, in this one, in particular, you see a very close relationship between, again, the influence of the galaxy, the galactic system, and how much glaciation and the motion of ice in the northern regions, and North Atlantic, in particular, as recorded by how much stuff it deposits in the ocean.

Again, another deviation, another anomaly. We're starting to see a pretty consistent and clear picture here.

We make a leap, a big leap, and we go to time-scales of not thousands of years, but millions, tens of millions,

Again, for our viewers who've been watching these shows, these are things we've covered before, but I wanted to go through this sequence, just to make it really clear that you see this on all these time-scales. You see this on time-scales of tens, and hundreds of millions of years, and variations of galactic influence, we see the imprints, the shadows, of that galactic influence embedded in climate records. Nested within that, on time-scales of thousands of years, we see variations in galactic influence imprinted on variations of measurements of the water cycle, glaciation, these things. And nested within that, on hundreds of years, you see the same thing. Within that, on decades, you see evidence for the same thing.

FIGURE 6

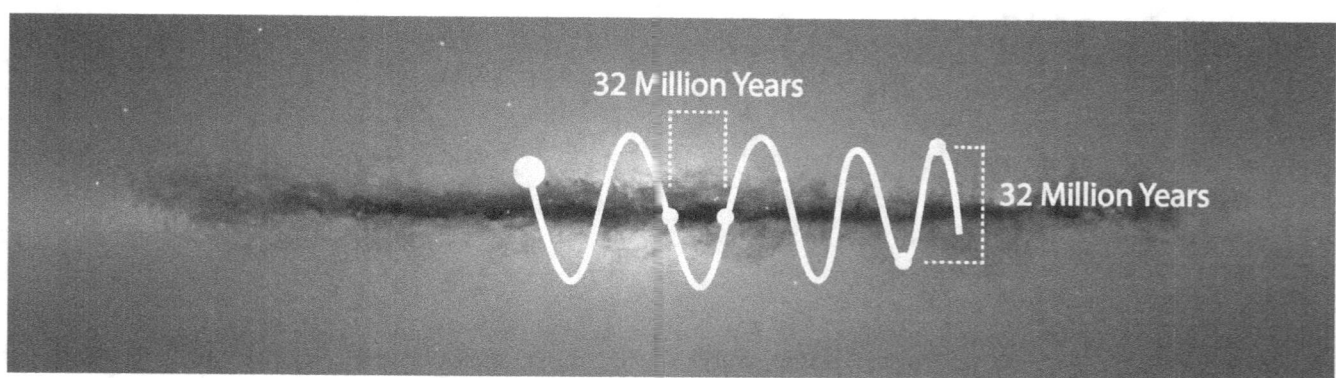

FIGURE 7

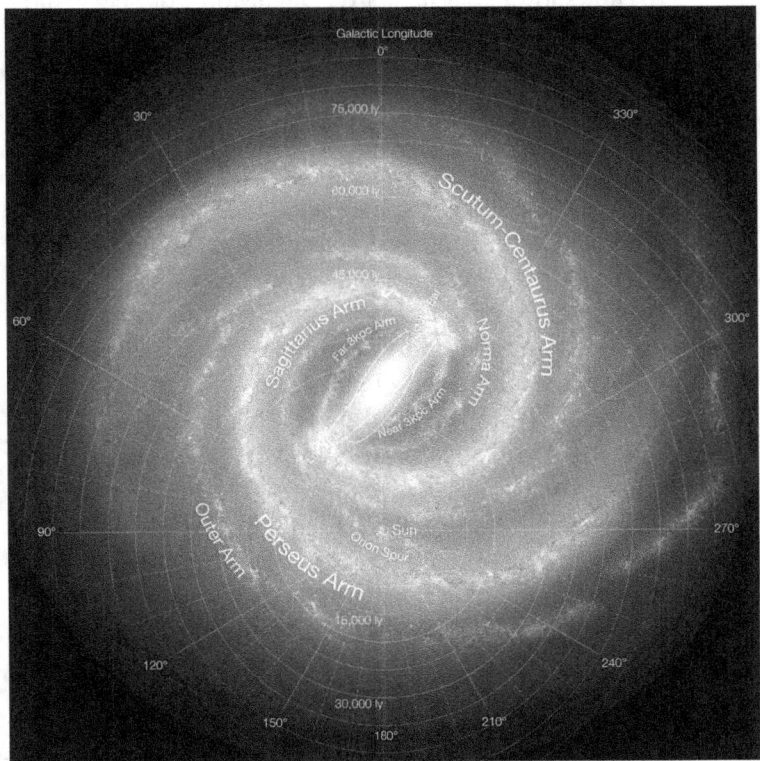

So you have this kind of nested system of deviations, variations, which all point to the role of galactic activity, as playing a major role in affecting how the Earth's atmospheric system, our water cycle, our water system, and the associated processes of climate and weather, are expressed.

Figure 7: This is our environment now. This is our starting place for understanding what is our environment. What are the environmental conditions that we're dealing with, that we want to improve and manage, as mankind? We have to start here now, looking at the galaxy.

Simulating Ionization: Svensmark's Study

Now, I want to go through something which I haven't gone through on these programs before, which is taking a further step in examining how this galactic influence is expressed in our atmospheric system, in particular. What is the nature of this expression of galactic activity, influencing and contributing to our climate, weather, water cycle systems, here on Earth? And the key to this, the main thing, is recognizing this continuous flux of high-energy radiation.

Again, this is something that's been known for over

a century now: that we're being flooded from all around, with high-energy radiation coming from beyond the Solar System, coming from the galaxy. And this is penetrating us right now. It's literally showering throughout the entire atmosphere. And the amount of this influence, again, varies with how active the Sun, how active the galaxy is, where in the galaxy we are, what type of galactic environment, but it's always there as a factor affecting the characteristics of the atmosphere.

And what we're most interested in here, right now, is how it affects the ionization characterization of the atmosphere.

So the atmosphere is mostly a neutral gas; it's not charged. If you want to take it in reductionist terms, all the molecules are balanced between their electrons and their protons. There's no charge to the atmosphere.

With the influence of this high-energy radiation from the galaxy, it has an effect of ionizing a certain portion of the atmosphere. It changes the characteristics; it changes the properties of the atmospheric system. Normally, minus the effects from the Earth and certain natural sources of radiation, much of the atmosphere would be neutral. It wouldn't be ionized at all. It wouldn't have any of these ionization effects from the galaxy.

We have this constant input from the galactic system, which is creating a certain level of ionization, and that affects all kinds of things. That affects how the global electric circuit operates. We're starting to realize that it actually affects how lightning occurs, a fascinating thing—kind of a side note. But what we want to home in on here, is that this ionization effect, the creation of these charged ions in the atmosphere, actually plays a very significant role in influencing and controlling how water behaves in the atmosphere. And this is critical.

And to illustrate some of this, because this is still something of a hotly debated topic, I want to go through a couple of experiments that illustrate this process: that ionization actually plays a key role in affecting how water vapor behaves in the atmospheric system.

So again, the Sun has pumped the atmosphere full of water vapor. It has evaporated water, and changed it from a liquid state, to a gas state, and filled the atmo-

FIGURE 8

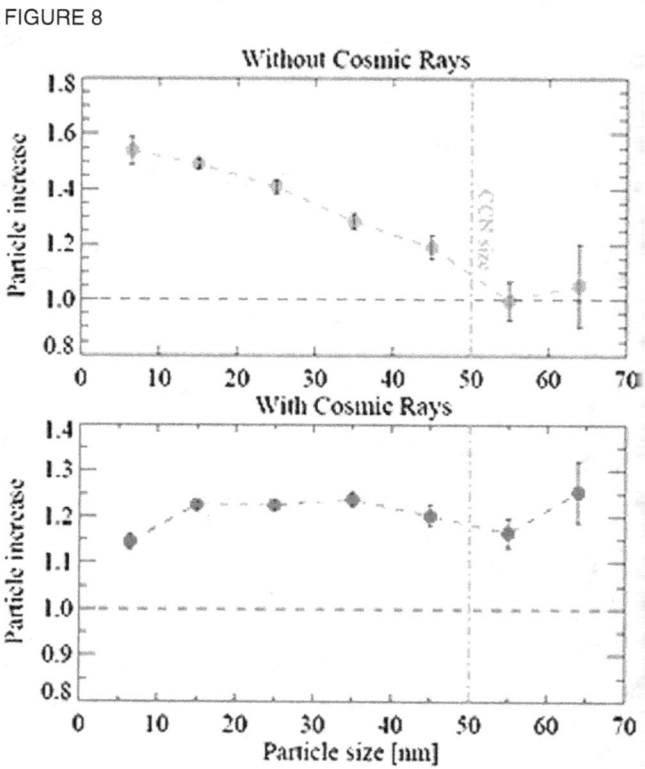

Without Cosmic Rays

With Cosmic Rays

Particle size [nm]

sphere with water vapor. But then we're seeing that the galactic influence plays a critical role in affecting and determining how that water vapor behaves when it's in the atmospheric system, by controlling the properties and characteristics of the atmospheric system. It creates a galactic environment, within which the water system acts, and reacts, and expresses itself.

Let's go through a couple of experiments investigating these properties.

This is a study by the Danish professor [Henrik] Svensmark (**Figure 8**), illustrating the role of ionization, simulating the effect of high-energy ionization, high-energy radiation, from the galaxy, and showing experimentally, that with an increase in the ionization effect, an increase of galactic, cosmic radiation, you get an increase in the growth of aerosols, and the condensation of water vapor, to lay the basis for cloud formation.

So again, go back to the earlier graphic (Figure 3) I showed, of the cosmic ray flux and the cloud cover changing, in direct relationship to each other. This was an experiment demonstrating some of the underlying physics of that: that when you get an increased ionization effect, you get the formation of the constituent parts of clouds. You accelerate the ability for clouds to form, by creating these little aerosols, and particles that grow

to become the basis for the formation of cloud droplets. They show experimentally: On the top, you see, without the effect of cosmic rays, the size—the horizontal scale is the size of the particles, the aerosols. So, without the role of cosmic rays, you see the number of them declining, as the size grows. They're not growing to the size where they can be the basis for cloud formation.

In the bottom graphic, in the blue, you see, with the influence of cosmic rays—a simulated effect, similar to cosmic rays—you see that, as the particle size grows, the number of the particles continues to increase. You get more of these larger particles, which lay the basis for the formation of clouds. And this vertical red line here, is kind of a cut-off point where you start to reach a certain critical size, which is very, very important for the formation of clouds.

So, you start to get the buildup of these things to a certain size, where they can start to form clouds. And you see that, again, without the role of a simulated galactic ray influence, the size drops off; the amount of these things drops off, as you approach that critical size.

But when you do introduce the role of a simulated galactic influence, the ionization effects of galactic cosmic radiation, you continue to get a production of these particles, up to this critical size and beyond it.

So this is one experiment demonstrating that the role—again, we're looking at what is the nature of the influence of this galactic effect on the atmosphere. Here we're seeing indications of how the galactic influence, the ionization effect, directly helps to facilitate processes leading to cloud formation, which involves, again, how water vapor behaves in the atmosphere, the kind of collection and dispersal of evaporated molecules of water to form clusters, and eventually droplets. So again, the role of cosmic rays affecting directly how this process occurs.

So, this is one experiment which demonstrated this process.

Other Ionization Experiments

Another experiment approached it in a different way, taking on a little bit of a different question (**Figure 9**). Not concerned so much with cloud formation, particularly, but just concerned with the process of condensation of water vapor, in particular. And in this case, they were interested in the ionizing effects of radon, which is a radioactive gas. How the ionizing effects of radioactive radon help to facilitate the process of the condensation of water vapor. And, in particular here, they're more

FIGURE 9

Laboratory experiments on radon 222 exposure effects on local environmental temperature: implications for satellite TIR measurements

Martinelli G., Solecki A.T., Tchorz-Trzeciakiewicz D.E.,
Piekarz M., Grudzinska K.K.

giovannimartinelli@arpa.emr.it

interested in how this effect actually relates to the precursors to earthquakes, but that's a second subject. We already have plenty to go through today.

But what they're looking at here was, you add a source of ionization—in this case, radon, instead of galactic cosmic rays. They were able to measure the increase of the condensation of water vapor. So again, we're looking at how these conditions of the atmosphere, governed by ionization, how that affects how water behaves. And in the large, how the water cycle behaves in the atmosphere.

And they showed, that when you increased the ionization with radon, in this case, you get a slight, but clear decrease in humidity, so the water, instead of being dispersed as vapor throughout the chamber, starts to condense, and you get lower humidity measured. And they also measured a slight increase in temperature, which is associated, again, with this condensation process.

This is an important factor. The Sun puts in a huge amount of energy to evaporate ocean water, and when that water is in a vaporous state, when it's evaporated, it has some extra energy to it. When it condenses back to liquid, when it changes from a gas state back to a liquid state, it re-releases that energy as heat. Sometimes you've heard of this as latent heat release.

Figure 10: So, here we see a relatively small, but clearly identifiable increase in temperature, in this relatively small experiment, showing that latent heat has been released, and water is being condensed. So again, a second experiment showing us that these ionization effects are important factors telling us how water behaves in the atmosphere.

We have a third experiment, which shows this in an even different way, an independent way (**Figure 11**). In

FIGURE 10

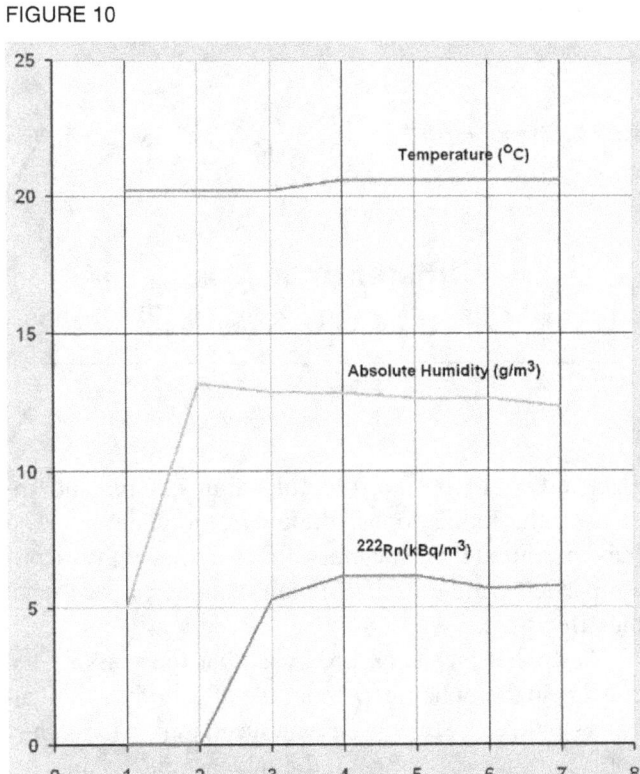

this experiment, they used electricity to generate the ionization effect. So, we're looking at these different sources of ionization: galactic/cosmic rays; radon; now electricity. And what they show here (**Figure 12**), in my very simplified illustration—just to try to show the basics of what they did—they ran a high-voltage current through a needle, which discharged some of the

FIGURE 11

Poster for the 54th ASMS Conference on Mass Spectrometry, Seattle, Washington, USA (2006)

The effect of needle voltage on the negative ion formation using atmospheric pressure corona discharge ionization (APCDI) in air

Kanako Sekimoto, Mitsuo Takayama

International Graduate School of Arts and Sciences, Yokohama City University, Yokohama, Japan

FIGURE 12

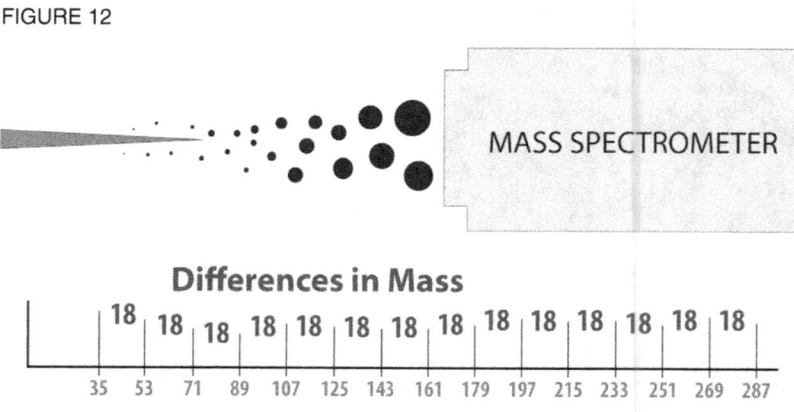

MASS SPECTROMETER

Differences in Mass

| | 18 | 18 | 18 | 18 | 18 | 18 | 18 | 18 | 18 | 18 | 18 | 18 | 18 | 18 | |
| 35 | 53 | 71 | 89 | 107 | 125 | 143 | 161 | 179 | 197 | 215 | 233 | 251 | 269 | 287 |

Mass of Individual Clusters

electricity into the surrounding atmosphere, and increased the ionization of the air in the chamber. And they measured then, the mass, the weights, of the different particles and clusters in their chamber, to see what the effect was.

And what they measured was that the mass of the clusters in their chamber, under the effect of this ionization—in this case, electrically induced ionization—they got clear, discrete jumps in the increase of the mass of the clusters. And those jumps were of the atomic mass of 18, which is the mass of a water molecule. So they were able to directly measure the increase of the mass of these clusters, in steps which were, in effect, the measurement of each water molecule jumping onto the cluster. And they showed that when you increase the ionization, now you see an increase in number of water molecules condensing, onto larger and larger clusters, growing clusters.

So, three different experiments, kind of taking different approaches, utilizing different sources of ionization, all pointing to the same results: that the ionization conditions of the atmosphere play a critical role in affecting how water behaves in the atmospheric system. How the water cycle expresses itself in the atmosphere.

So, in effect, what we're doing with these things, we're kind of playing with the cosmic environment of the atmosphere. The atmosphere in a certain condition, a certain environment—certain conditions of that are created by this galactic influence. And these experiments were playing with that type of influence, were modulating that cosmic environment called the atmospheric system, and demonstrating and showing that we change how water behaves, or acts, under these conditions.

So these are three controlled experiments, showing that the behavior of the atmosphere of water vapor, that the behavior of atmospheric water vapor is directly responding to this ionization effects.

Cosmic Ray Flux

But we also see direct evidence of this, in a much larger experiment, which is the whole planet, when we measure the effects of variations in ionization, variations in the amount of galactic influence, and we can measure changes in certain properties or expressions of how the water behaves in the atmosphere.

Here we have a rather fascinating illustration (**Figure 13**), where the scientists looked at periods when you get a very sharp reduction in the flux of galactic activity. These are attributed to when the Sun—the Sun is kind of a wily figure, it's doing stuff, surprising us, doing different things. Sometimes the Sun releases very large explosions of plasma, of activity, that can kind of sweep past the Earth. And they can temporarily increase the shielding of the entire Earth system from this galactic influence.

FIGURE 13

GALACTIC COSMIC RAYS AND CLOUDS

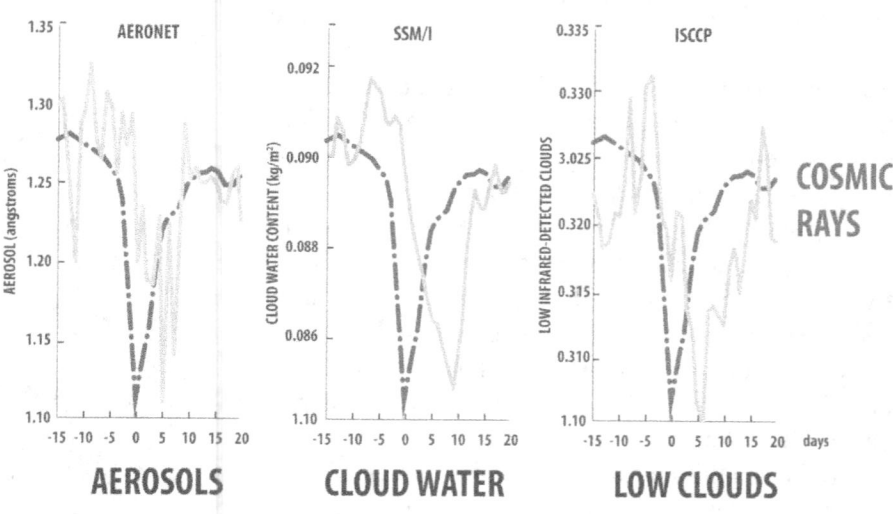

AERONET · AEROSOLS

SSM/I · CLOUD WATER

ISCCP · LOW CLOUDS

COSMIC RAYS

As a result, what we measure on Earth, is a very sharp reduction in the amount of galactic cosmic rays. So on Earth, we see this Solar outburst, this coronal mass ejection, shooting past us. We see a sharp reduction in the amount of galactic influence, and what these scientists did, was they took five of the largest of these events, the largest of these sharp drops in cosmic ray flux (these are technically called Forbush decreases—named after the guy who found this relationship). So they took five of these largest events, and showed that by then looking at satellite measurements, and various conditions in the at-

FIGURE 14

Short-Term Correlation of Temperature in the Stratosphere and Secondary Cosmic Rays

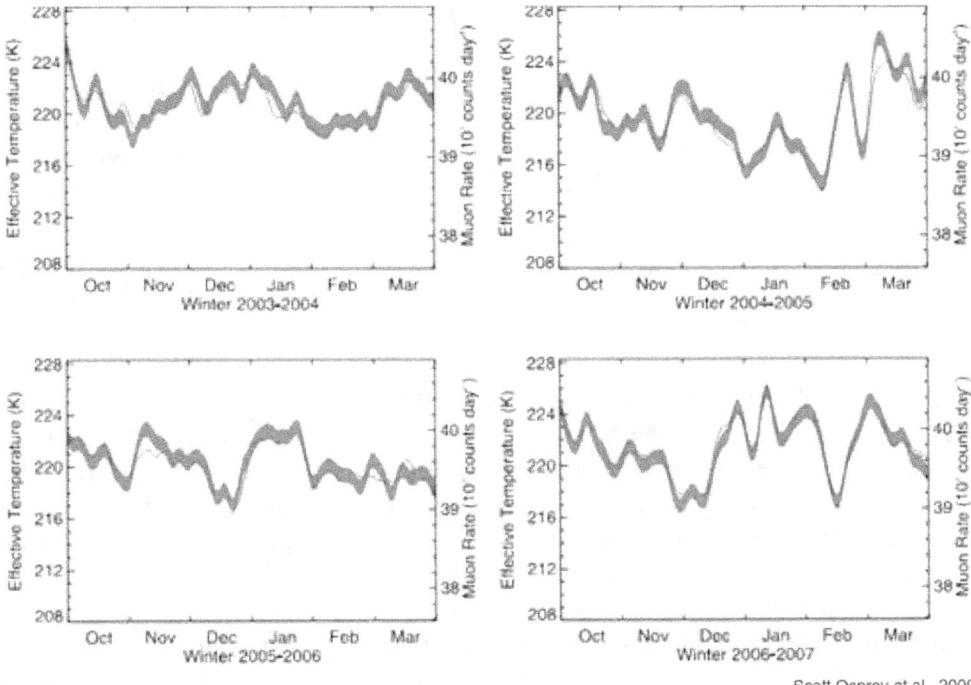

Scott Osprey et al., 2009

mosphere, you get a direct correspondence in a variation in how the water is behaving in the atmosphere, following these decreases in cosmic ray flux, decreases in the resulting ionization effects.

On the far left: In each of these, the dotted-dash line, the purple line, is the cosmic ray flux. So, it's the same for all of these. You see the sharp drop in the amount of cosmic rays. But then on the right, you also see a corresponding drop a couple of days later, of the amount of aerosols in the atmosphere, pointing us back to this earlier experiment by Svensmark, the Danish experiment showing that the aerosol formation is directly influenced by the effects of cosmic rays.

So, as we would expect, we see a decrease in the aerosol formation in the atmosphere, as measured by satellites.

We also see, a couple of days after the decrease in cosmic ray flux, a decrease in the amount of water measured in clouds. So the amount of water being condensed and forming and building up in clouds, decreases. Again, consistent with what we were just looking at, what these experiments showed us.

And then we also see a decrease in low-level cloud cover generally, the third graphic there, another confir-

mation, indicating this relationship between cosmic ray flux and cloud formation. That condensation of water vapor, the formation of aerosols, the amount of water condensing on these aerosols is an expression of this cosmic environment, so to speak.

Figure 14: Here we have another independent indication of this process. These are a little bit hard to see, because the correlation is so good. You see a very clear correlation between the variations in temperature, up in the stratosphere, and variations in cosmic ray flux.

Now again, coming back to what I was saying earlier, when you increase the rate of condensation of water vapor, you release heat. So it makes sense that if we get variations in the amount of cosmic radiation, varying the amount of condensation of water vapor, you get a direct relationship to how much heat is released in the process.

Again, a very clear correlation. You can't even really tell that it's two lines, because they line up so well. You kind of see some deviation in it in a couple of them. You get this very clear relationship between cosmic ray flux, and temperature, because again, cosmic rays are governing the rate of condensation, and the rate of release of latent heat.

FIGURE 15

Available online at www.sciencedirect.com

ScienceDirect

ELSEVIER

Advances in Space Research xxx (2008) xxx–xxx

ADVANCES IN
SPACE
RESEARCH
(a COSPAR publication)

www.elsevier.com/locate/asr

Solar, geomagnetic and cosmic ray intensity changes, preceding
the cyclone appearances around Mexico

J. Pérez-Peraza [a,*], S. Kavlakov [b], V. Velasco [a], A. Gallegos-Cruz [c], E. Azpra-Romero [d],
O. Delgado-Delgado [d], F. Villicaña-Cruz [d]

[a] Instituto de Geofísica, Universidad Nacional Autónoma de México, C.U., Coyoacán, 04510 México, D.F., Mexico
[b] Bulgarian Academy of Sciences, Galileo Galilei Str. 17/B, 1113, Sofia, Bulgaria
[c] UPIICSA, I.P.N., Depto. de Ciencias Básicas, Té 950, Iztacalco, 08400 México, D.F., Mexico
[d] Centro de la Atmosfera, Universidad Nacional Autónoma de México, C.U., Coyoacán, 04510 México, D.F., Mexico

Received 28 November 2006; received in revised form 21 November 2007; accepted 7 December 2007

Figure 15: There's one other study to cite in the process, which is a paper written by scientists in Mexico, showing that there's a clear relationship between the variations in cosmic ray flux, and the formation of cyclones and hurricanes, and their strength, their intensity. So, another pretty fascinating relationship.

One mechanism that's been proposed to help to illustrate this, goes to this release of latent heat process. Cosmic ray flux is an important factor facilitating condensation, releasing latent heat, and that helps to warm the upper atmosphere. So, if you get sharp variations in the amount of warming of the upper atmosphere, you can get sharp changes in the temperature difference, between the ocean and the upper atmosphere, which can increase or decrease the convection rate, which is critical in helping cyclones form, or grow in strength. I'm covering this pretty quickly, but again, we see evidence that, in studying a number of cyclone formations, and when they occur, they see that they tend to occur after you have these sharp variations in the cosmic ray flux.

The Next Step: Managing the Galaxy

So, that's a lot, I know. We ran through a bunch of things on these variations on these long time-scales, but also these experiments and these studies indicating just how much the galactic environment is constantly an active factor in determining the conditions here on Earth.

What we have to take out of this, is that we are living in a galactic environment (Figure 7). We're literally living in a galactic atmosphere. This cosmic ray flux is the expression of the galactic system. It doesn't end on the outskirts of our Solar System. It comes in, it's there, it's everywhere, and it's shaping certain critical characteristics of the atmosphere. And these characteristics, as

we just went through these studies to show, play a critical role in determining how the water cycle behaves; how atmospheric water vapor behaves; cloud formation; temperature of the atmosphere. Even such things as strong as cyclones and hurricanes are indeed, at least in part, expressions of the activity of this galactic factor.

So, the conditions which we exist in, which we're living in, are driven by, again, not just the Sun-Earth interaction, but are caught in this galactic influence. We see the indications of the principle of the galactic system as a whole, is an active factor in shaping and determining the environment in which we live. And I think for today, we'll leave it there.

What that brings it to, which is what I think we'll get into next week, is a discussion of how we can then manage that. What we're seeing here is all these kinds of shadows, experiments, illustrations. The point is not to get caught up in the details of any one of these, but to paint this broad picture, paint this specific picture, that we're living in a galactic environment; but it's a galactic environment that we can actually manage and control, which we can get into next week. And that is what will enable us to control the water cycle in a completely new way.

We've talked about these so-called ionization systems being used to create rainfall, to create canals in the sky of water vapor, to move water vapor in the sky, to where we want it. To induce it to fall where we want it. To begin to control various aspects of the weather, control various aspects of the water cycle, by managing what is really the galactic, cosmic environment of our own atmospheric system. With an understanding of these processes, these relationships, and the role they play in shaping the quality of the atmosphere, that determines how the water cycle behaves, we can act in that domain.

Next week, I think it would be good to go through some details of that process, and some of the experiments that have occurred—directly controlling weather, increasing rainfall, and some of the potential of these systems. But this is where we have to go. And under this type of program, California, other places, we can solve these droughts. We have the potential to do these types of things. But it's moving to this higher insight into managing the galactic, cosmic environment of the atmosphere, which gives us this highest potential.

So, that can be kind of a teaser for next week, to get into what we can begin to do with these systems.

American astronaut Stephen Robinson takes a walk off the Space Shuttle to the International Space Station in 2005.

NASA

There Is Plenty of Water

Liona Fan-Chiang: I think the breakthrough will be not just being able to solve droughts. We'll be able to see droughts as almost an arcane word, in the sense that, as you said, this idea of a water crisis is a misnomer. Because there's no lack of water. Actually, you had this funny number, I thought. You said there were trillions of times [the amount] of water in some other galaxy?

Deniston: They measured the amount of galaxy water coming out of the different galactic systems, and they came up with 140 trillion times the amount of water on Earth. So, water's not exactly a rare commodity in our universe.

Fan-Chiang: So, the idea of being able to—well, first of all, you mentioned the ionization systems, which I guess we'll go through next time, but these experiments also show that we can directly influence these processes, and that the processes are all interconnected. And so, the idea of just treating a land drought, separately, or even rain, or even weather, separately, seems like a very *old* idea. It will become as ancient as the rain dance.

Beets: I think that gets to the larger point about this process of the human species. You know, Mr. LaRouche said something yesterday that I found so striking. He said that—it's a terrible paraphrase, but something to

the effect of, man, as he understands himself now, is merely a projection, a shadow, of what mankind actually is. And it's that tantalizing existence above, which is projecting down on what we think our power is now, that we should reach for, and learn to discover, that has to guide the actions of nations and scientists and leaders today. It's just the temptation of discovering the true higher nature of man, and in that processing, *creating* the true and higher nature of man.

I was thinking back to Kepler. Before Kepler, the Solar System was not a physical system; it was not something you interact with. It was something you observed. And for the first time, with Kepler, it became a physical system, which means what? That we could eventually manage it. And there's more to the Solar System, clearly, than what Kepler knew 400 years ago, but we're filling out what he unleashed, and that's exactly what you're beginning with this galactic system. It's that we have to turn it into a *human* system, a physical system.

Clearly, with these initial steps in understanding this electrical-ionization characteristic of the atmosphere as a whole, and then, being able to create mimic effects, but also create new effects—that perhaps the galactic system doesn't do explicitly—we're beginning to bend and manage, and could yoke and harness this galactic force, and turn it into, shape it into something which is a human power.

Fan-Chiang: Yes. And it really does point out that we've already become a global species. That's already occurred. Vernadsky pointed it out, at the beginning of World War I. And we're very, very slowly becoming a Solar System species.

But, you're right. Kepler already laid out the boundaries. He already laid out the fact that we are a Solar System species, and in some sense, already laid out the galactic [principle] too. But, I think that is going to be a *huge* point of contention—or it is already a huge point of contention: which is, that we not only already live in the galactic process, but that we *can*, and therefore must, control it.

That's really going to be a huge point—we have to take that on very strongly. Because not only the idea that these correlations exist, can be proved scientifically, and so on, but the fact that we have to control it, is going to be a moral question. And that's really—that determines everything.

Redefining Mankind

Deniston: That goes back to this point about redefining what mankind is. Again, we went through a lot of detail here today, because I thought it was important to put this on the record, and give something for people to chew on. But the point is to work through this, and come out of it with a single conception. And the challenge is to see this—you see effects, you see shadows. But what governs those is principles—single, defined principles. You see the water cycle, as we experience it is a shadow and effect of the intersection of the galactic interacting with the Solar System: the principle of the galactic system as a unity, interacting with the Solar System, and the processes on Earth.

The scientific concepts of biogeochemist Vladimir Vernadsky—the initiator of the idea of the Biosphere—whose concept of the "Noösphere," has been cited and further developed by Lyndon LaRouche.

THE ECONOMICS OF THE NOÖSPHERE

Lyndon H. LaRouche, Jr.

And the effects you see of that, are shadows created by those principles, those activities.

Mankind, in moving to manage these things in the way we're talking about—it's creating new shadows, which are on the scale of the galactic system, in effect. We're talking about looking at beginning to operate on a galactic level. People are so brainwashed, in terms of thinking of things in reductionist terms, in sense-perceptual terms. You talk about operating on a galactic level, they imagine you have to be like buzzing around from star to star, or something.

That's not how mankind operates. It's not about these reductionist terms, these sense-perceptual terms. It's about the principles governing the processes that we experience as shadows. We're seeing that these phenomena are shadows of a galactic principle, and we're demonstrating that mankind uniquely can see behind the shadows, can generate a conception of what the principle is, but then generate his own effects, his own shadows, which correspond to a uniquely creative mental relationship to the universe, on a galactic level.

Our relationship to the universe, under this type of direction, is a galactic relationship. That doesn't mean we're flying around the galaxy doing things. It means that mentally, creatively, again, we're subsuming any animal, biological capabilities of just the human biology, and we're going to a level of the principle of the galactic system, and then changing our behavior and operating from that standpoint.

Fan-Chiang: One of the things that Mr. LaRouche brought up yesterday was this idea that individuals can have an effect on, for example, the species as a whole, through the human mind. And people know that you can have a global effect, without being everywhere on the globe at once, or ever. You could have never traveled to places on the globe, and still have a global effect.

And that is something that is a process of evolution. We create conditions such that each individual can have an ability to have more and more of an effect on a larger and larger process. And that's the process of evolution, of mankind. And create societies such that individuals can have an effect in that way.

Beets: In transforming the species as a whole. And then each individual can express that new higher characteristic.

Fan-Chiang: This is the next step. Where each individual is acting on a galactic scale.

Beets: I think that's a great place to leave it for this week.

'You Can Take Water from the Ocean, And Create Precipitation' on the Land

Professor Pulinets was interviewed on April 30, 2015 by Benjamin Deniston.

The graphics in this article are still images from animations; to view those animations, see the interview video.

Benjamin Deniston: Hello, my name is Benjamin Deniston, with the LaRouche Political Action Committee Scientific Research Team, and I'm very happy to be joined today with Prof. Sergey Pulinets, speaking to us from Moscow over Google Hangouts, for a very special interview discussion on the subject of technologies that can be used to control weather and increase rainfall, to

BueSo TV

Prof. Sergey Pulinets, of the Space Research Institute at the Russian Academy of Sciences, presents his research at the 2011 European Geosciences Conference.

help address the drought and water crises going on in places like California, other places in the United States, but also other places around the world.

Obviously, this is a very important issue now, given the water shortage in the Western United States, but also globally, so we're very happy to be able to discuss some new technologies, new frontier ideas that can help mankind manage the atmospheric resources, the water resources of the sky, potentially, and begin to give mankind potentially an ability to increase rainfall where it is needed, and secure the water supplies for various regions.

Professor Pulinets has some important background and familiarity with these technologies and some of the theories behind how these technologies work to allow mankind to stimulate rainfall with ionization systems. Professor Pulinets has been involved with a company in the United States called Rain on Request, which is promoting the utilization of these technologies in the United States. He's also written on the subject, includ-

ing an article that was published in *Russia Beyond the Headlines* in 2009, entitled "Weather Control? Yes, It Is Really Possible."

Earlier, Professor Pulinets had worked as part of a team assessing the validity and scientific basis for some of these weather control systems in Mexico, in the late '90s and early 2000s.

So again, I'm very happy to be joined by Dr. Pulinets today. This is going to be a very useful and helpful discussion for this current water situation.

And to start off, I would like to ask you, Dr. Pulinets, because clearly this issue is met with a lot of skepticism; when you bring this up, a lot of people have a very quick reaction of just dismissing the idea that we can control things such as weather processes, rainfall; but you have done work actually assessing the scientific basis for some of these systems that have been operational for many years and which have been reported to show success in increasing rainfall in Mexico.

I was hoping we could start by hearing about the history of your familiarity with these systems, and your understanding of where they've worked and how well they've been successful so far.

Ionization

Prof. Sergey Pulinets: Hello Ben, hello to everybody. I would like to clarify a little bit the situation. Actually, my background is space physics. And new ideas appeared from the end of the '90s, when we started to learn about the effects in the ionosphere that are associated with earthquakes. It was very interesting how the information from the ground, and even underground, penetrates to our space, and started to develop a theory about this. And to do this I had to be involved in geophysics, in solid geophysics: What happens before the earthquakes.

And for the first time, I encountered the problem of the ionization which is created by radon emanating from the Earth's crust, and the increase of this emanation before earthquakes. Radon can produce the ionization of air near the ground surface, and then, after ion hydration and latent heat release, this heat propagates up to the upper layers of the atmosphere, up to the tropopause.

This is known from the effects of cosmic rays on atmosphere. Probably you know that the clouds which cover our planet, to a great extent, are formed due to galactic cosmic rays, which produce ionization and then the ions become the centers of water vapor condensation, and nucleation and formation of drops and clouds, which we see every day; and there is a correlation between the cloud coverage of our planet and the variations of the fluxes of cosmic rays.

So nature gives us the answer, that ionization can produce the nucleation. We have these examples from space, galactic cosmic rays, and from the ground, from the nature of radioactivity; and we can see, for example, the results of studies of Japanese scientists (**Figure 1**), who, through the discharge from the needle, created the flux of ions and put them in the mass spectrometer, and were able to see how the particles grow.

And if you look at the picture, you will see the distance between the sequential spectrum lines: In atomic mass, it is 18: It is the atomic mass of the water molecule. And you see how the ions gain more and more and more water molecules, and it was proved experimentally. So this is, let's say, the theoretical background,

FIGURE 1

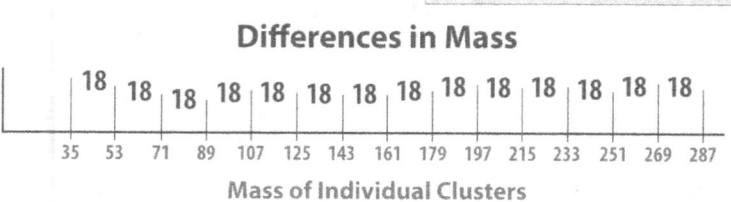

Differences in Mass

| 18 | 18 | 18 | 18 | 18 | 18 | 18 | 18 | 18 | 18 | 18 | 18 | 18 | 18 |

35 53 71 89 107 125 143 161 179 197 215 233 251 269 287

Mass of Individual Clusters

how the ionization can produce the large clusters, where in the center we have the ion and the envelope from the water molecules.

Mexico's ELAT

I came to Mexico and was working in the Institute of Geophysics of UNAM [National Autonomous University of Mexico]—the greatest university in Mexico City—working on the problem of earthquakes, but there I met some friends who made me familiar with a Mexican company named ELAT, which made experiments with the stimulation of rain. They had contracts with the governments of different states, especially in the drought areas of Mexico, such as in the Sonora desert, to produce rain to increase the harvest in these areas.

It is very interesting that the main idea, and maybe the ideology, was also proposed by a Russian scientist, Lev Pokhmelnykh, who was the founder of this company, and was supported by Mexican businessman Mario Dominguez, and primarily by the Mayor of Mexico City, Cuauhtémoc Cárdenas Solórzano. And because the physical mechanism is the same, simply the sources of ionization are different: We have radon before earthquakes; and they have a special installation which produces artificial ionization. So we started to cooperate.

I was familiar with their results: Actually I can provide you some pictures with their results, and they are very impressive.

After that, I became a member of the scientific committee of representatives of the Mexican meteorological agency scientists working in the physics of atmosphere; there was one scientist from the United States. I can give you the list of these scientists who were in-

FIGURE 2

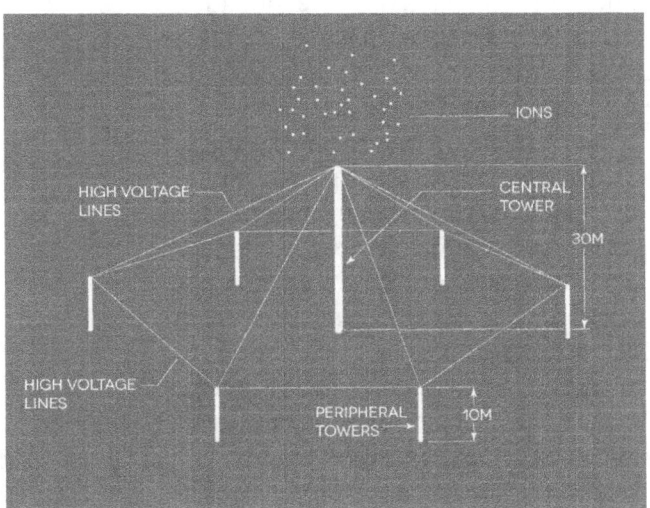

volved in this committee, who had the purpose to estimate whether the facts produced by this company are real. I participated in several meetings of this committee where we discussed their result.

So, how does this installation look? (**Figure 2**) It is an iron mast of nearly 30 meters, from which, like rays, very thin wires go. Why very thin? We know that if we take the needle, for example, before the thunderstorm, when we have high voltage, high electric field in the atmosphere, we sometimes can see the discharge from the needle. So now, let us imagine that we have the ends of the needle connected to the thin wire, and the smaller the diameter of this wire, the more effective is the growth of the coronal discharge, by putting the higher electrical voltage on this wire.

So you create something like an "umbrella" around this mast, and you have shorter peripheral masts around the umbrella's circumference (**Figure 2a**). So you have this installation, and the higher voltage which produces the ionization of air; and then, if you put positive or negative potential on this installation, with this electric field—for example, if you put positive potential, the positive ions will be moved by the electric field up to the upper layers; and moving to the upper layers, they gain more and more water molecules and become nuclei to form clouds.

FIGURE 3

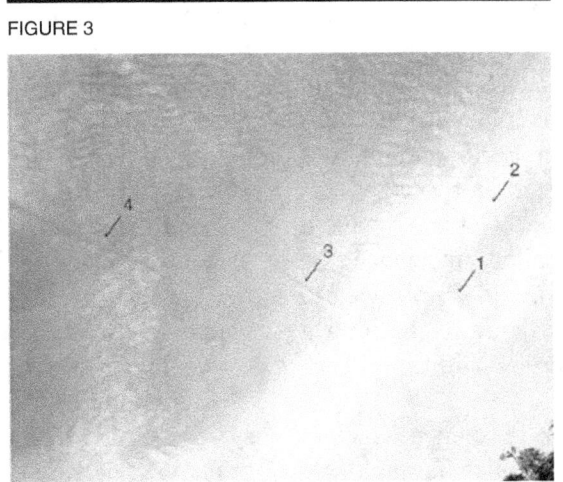

Actually, for example, we can see these effects even before earthquakes, when the linear clouds are formed, over the tectonic faults (**Figure 3**). And this effect is observed everywhere and reported by many scientists. This is the same effect of the electric field, of the ions produced by the ionization by radon, going up, and forming the linear clouds over the active tectonic fault.

This is the explanation of this technology. Of course, the physics stands behind this, but I should underline one very important thing: We know the technology of so-called cloud-seeding, when, from an airplane, you suspend, for example, silver iodine, or you can even suspend cement, plus any dust or aerosol in the air, which can become the center of condensation, and you stimulate the precipitation of rain.

But the difference between these two technologies is the following: By seeding, you can precipitate only the water which already exists in the air; you can create nothing more. But here, you create the new nucleus, and you take the water vapor and collect it into drops. And if you put your installation near the seashore—for example, in California, you can very easily put this installation near the shore—you can collect the humidity and then transport it, because you can put the different potentials between two installations. This creates movement of this air, filled by [these nuclei] for the formation of clouds inland (**Figure 4**).

Creating Precipitation

So actually, if we are now speaking of the technology, you can take water from the ocean, to move inland and then create precipitation. To create precipitation, you need to create some conditions, relationships between the temperature in the altitude of the clouds and dew temperature. So, you should have your temperature lower than the dew temperature, to condense; this creates the drops, and creates the kind of instability which, in nature, we have in thunderstorms.

Actually, all people, and sometimes physicists who study the atmosphere, think in terms of hydrodynamics. For example, describing typhoons, hurricanes, they look only at the hydrodynamic mechanical movement, but they forget that we are living in an electrical world: a huge electrical potential on the top of the hurricane.

We live in the constant electric field which exists between the ionosphere and the ground (**Figure 5**); the potential difference between the ionosphere and the ground is near 250 kilovolts, and sometimes it can gain 400-500 kilovolts. And on the ground surface, the vertical gradient of the electric field is 100 or 150 volts per meter. You're a tall guy, so between your legs and your head, you have a 200-volt potential difference all the time!

This potential difference is created by thunderstorm activity globally. Thunderstorms charge the ionosphere positively in relation to the Earth, and in areas of fair weather, we have the return to fair weather current, which is very low, but nevertheless, we have a closed electric circuit, which is called, in science, the "global electric circuit" (**Figure 6**). And simply, we use everything that is given to us by nature, helping a little bit with this ionization to create additional centers of nucleation.

Now, there exists a conception in science which is named "ion-induced nucleation," which is explosive

FIGURE 4

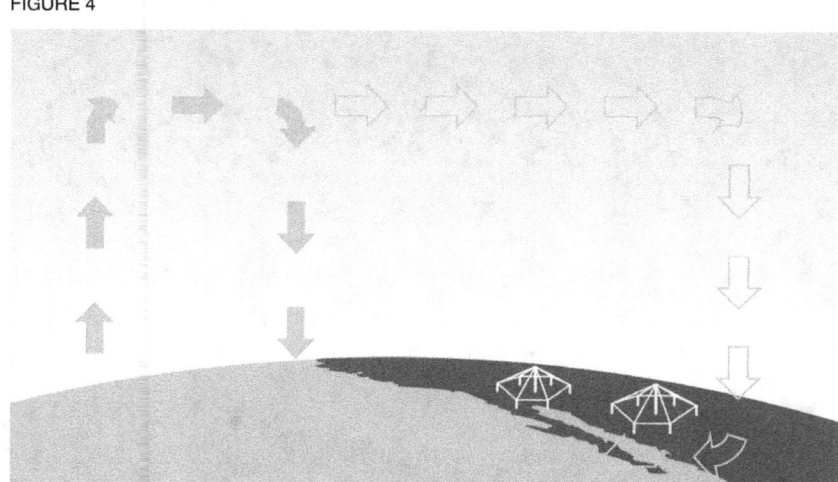

FIGURE 5

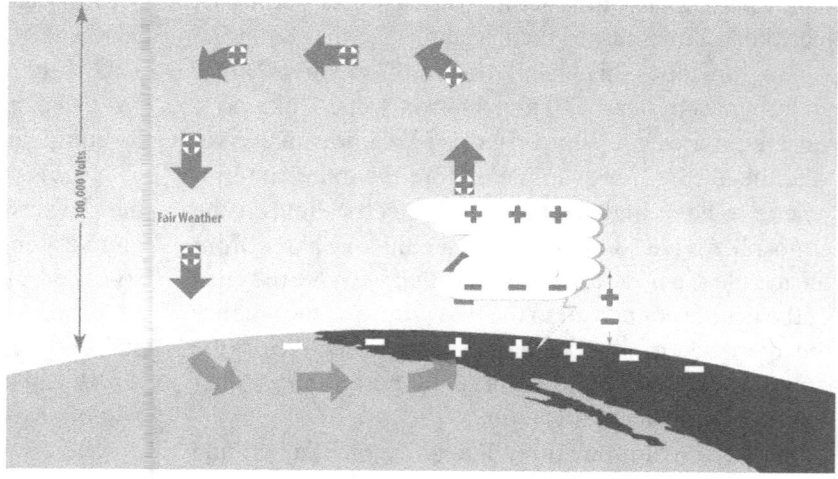

nucleation in the presence of the source of the ionization. So you can produce these centers of condensation, and your task is to transport it to the altitude of cloud formation, and then create the conditions to precipitate this.

Ion Hydration

Deniston: Just to clarify for our audience here, let's take a couple of steps back: You're saying, we start with the fact that on the one side, there's already a lot of water vapor, evaporated water in the atmosphere...

Pulinets: Yes.

Deniston: So on the one side, with these ionization systems, you can create the conditions which accelerate or increase the rate at which that evaporated water con-

FIGURE 6

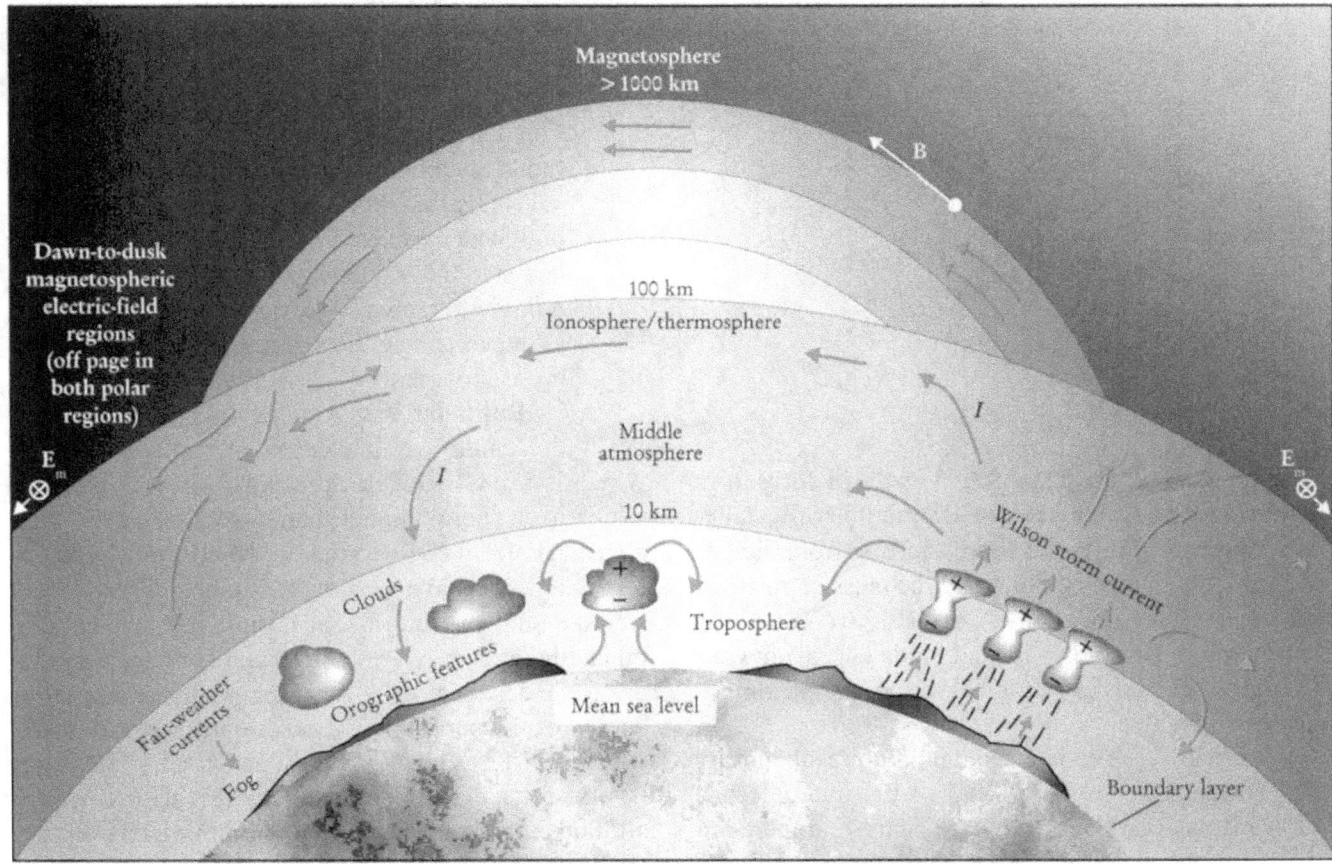

denses and forms liquid droplets, which can help...

Pulinets: The initial state is not droplets yet, but nucleation centers. They are too small to call them droplets. It is a complex process, from the ion to a larger particle, to the ion cluster, then nucleation, and then the droplet. The same process as formation of clouds in natural conditions: Simply, you form nuclei near the ground surface, and then transport them up with an electric field.

Deniston: And you had said that Japanese scientists have done experiments demonstrating the role of increased ionization in facilitating this process.

Pulinets: Yes. Yes, they published several papers, and I can provide you these publications with the figures, showing how these particles grow. It is very interesting.

I should also underline, that, contrary to the pure condensation, which needs saturated water vapor, 100% humidity, pure water, to have condensation, this process is called "ion hydration," attachment of the water molecules to the ion. And you can see from their pictures that this process takes place in *any* level of relative humidity, even if you have 25% humidity, you still will have the formation of these ion clusters with attached water molecules. Of course, the higher the humidity, the more effective the process we have, the larger the particles are formed. But in general, hydration takes place at *any level of humidity*. Even in low humidity conditions, you can create large particles and precipitate them in the form of dew, for example.

And for the plants, it doesn't matter whether you have rain or if you have dew; they can gain water even from dew.

Inducing Water from the Ocean

Deniston: You had also said, in addition to helping to induce what atmospheric moisture is there to come down, either to precipitate or to form as dew, you can also induce more flows of moisture to come in from over the ocean, you can actually increase the water availability in the atmosphere, too.

FIGURE 7

Pulinets: Yes. And I provided you the pictures from the Mexican experiments: You see the line of installations, perpendicular to the shore, starting from the Pacific, and this line helped to move the mass of air filled with the humidity inland in Mexico (**Figure 7**).

Deniston: And so, you had said, based on your work, these systems in Mexico have shown some pretty impressive results.

Pulinets: Yes. You can see there, the results of the filling of dams [reservoirs—ed.] of the hydroelectric power plants. And there were two dams, and there are results for one and a half years, and you can see how these dams were filled up with this technology (**Figure 8**). Actually, they also tried to fight forest fires in the Yucatan Peninsula, creating artificial rain, to fight forest fires.

Deniston: And they also had success in doing that?

Pulinets: Yes, there are some statistical results showing the occurrence of forest fires during the period of the activity. You may have something like 20-30% increase of precipitation—not that you create heavy rains, you see, but you can increase, in an essential manner, the amount of water precipitated.

Deniston: Maybe to step back also—you had said early on that this is very similar to what occurs naturally with the radiation coming in from the galactic system. And I think we could take a few minutes to discuss that, because that is a relatively a new area of study, where we're starting to learn and understand the effects of what the Sun is doing, and then also, the effects of the high-energy radiation from the galaxy, are actually a constant input shaping the environment of the atmosphere, affecting climate, weather; affecting how water moves through the water cycle. You had said that the basis of these ionization technologies, is actually acting on a very similar area as the ionizing effects of the galaxy. Can you say more about that?

Pulinets: Yes. Any particle with energy—the energy of ionization of molecules of air which is from 10-15 electron volts—so any particles which have energy higher than this energy, can ionize a water molecule. If we stick to the cosmic sources of ionization, we have two main sources: There is our star, the Sun; and the galactic cosmic rays, which have much higher energy. And the altitude of penetration of these particles into the atmosphere depends on the energy of the particles. The solar particles have lower energy, so they cannot actually penetrate to the lower layers of the atmosphere, and they lose their energy at altitudes, say, from tens to hundreds kilometers (**Figure 9a**): This is the source of the Northern Lights. They excite the molecules, and atoms, actually—at these altitudes we are now speaking about atoms of oxygen and nitrogen, and we see the green and red lines of the polar lights (**Figure 9b**).

FIGURE 8

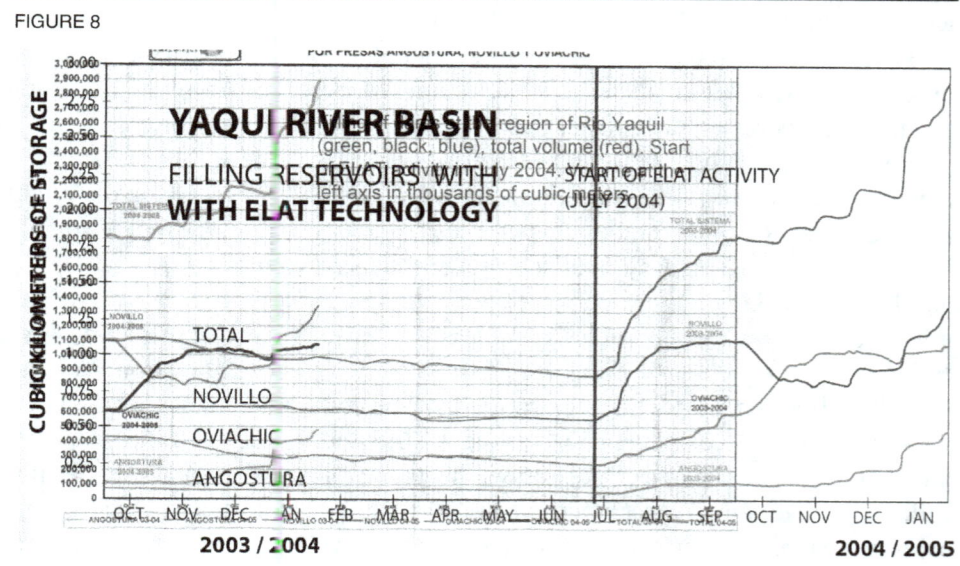

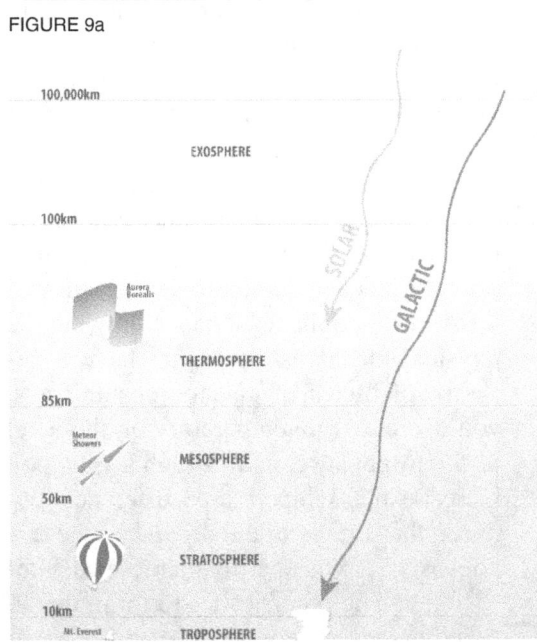

But the galactic cosmic rays, which have much higher energy, have the altitude peak where they lose their main energy, at the altitude of the tropopause, which is from 10-15 km. This is the altitude of the top of the clouds of our atmosphere (Figure 9a). So these are the layers where the clouds are formed, and the first good statistical results were made by [Henrik] Svensmark; he is a Danish scientist, who showed that during two cycles of the Sun's activity, 22 years, the cross-correlation coefficient was near 95% between the variations of the galactic cosmic rays' fluxes and the cloud coverage of our planet (**Figure 10**).

And now this theory has been developed very well, showing how the primary ions are formed; then they enter into the chemical reaction, create the final ions, and these final ions become hydrated and form the nucleus of clouds.

So this theory is well-developed, and probably you have heard of a large—huge, you can say!—chamber created at CERN, in Switzerland, where they studied this process of cloud formation. But they spent a lot of money, and I prefer the experiment of the Japanese, which is a very simple one, very clever, showing this process very clearly.

Latent Heat

And what is very interesting, is that sometimes physicists who are working in this field do not take into account another effect connected to this ionization: the release of latent heat. You know that water molecules free in the air, with the air existing as a gas, and water molecules in water, have different energies. Water can exist in three phases: It is gas, liquid, and solid. So, water vapor, water that we drink, and ice. And between them, there is a difference in the energy of the water molecules which we do not see; that's why we call it "latent heat" (**Figure 11**).

So, for example, to evaporate—you know, this is a proverb, that "a watched pot will never boil." Because it seems that you have reached 100° centigrade temperature, but you wait and wait and wait until the vapor starts to be emitted from the water. This is the period when the water molecules gain this latent heat to evaporate, to become free from the water. And we have a backward [reverse—ed.] process: When the water is condensed, it releases heat into the environment (Figure 11).

FIGURE 10

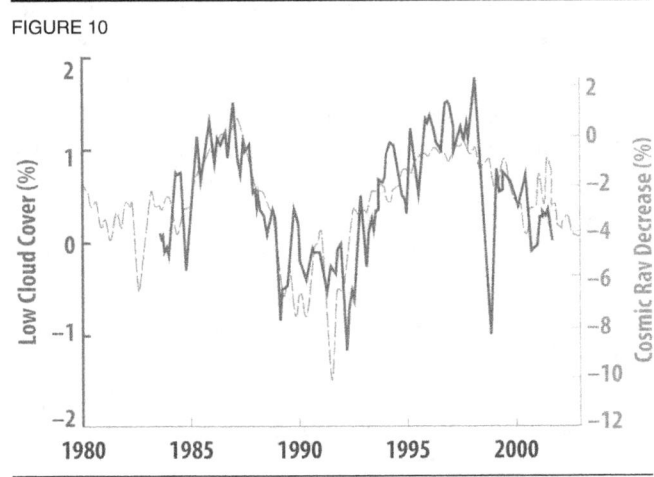

adapted from Marsh and Svensmark 2000

FIGURE 11

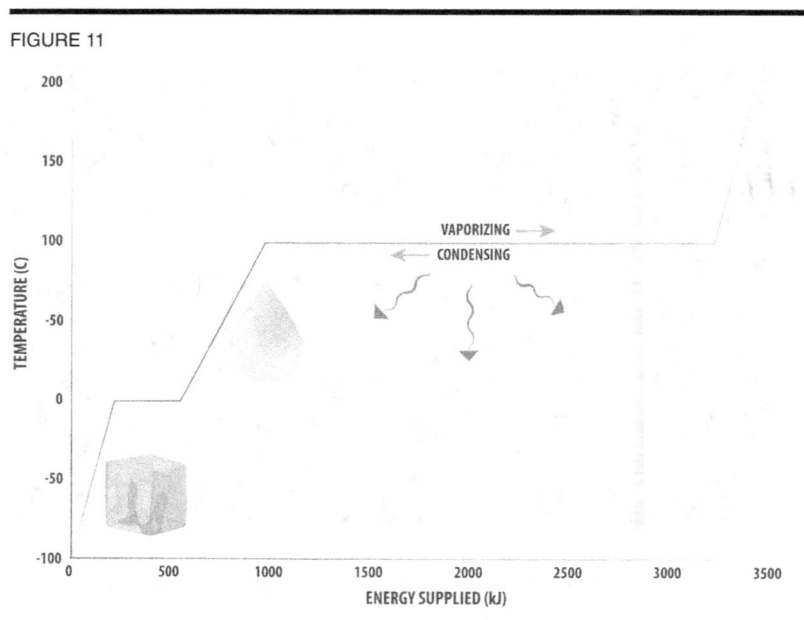

FIGURE 12

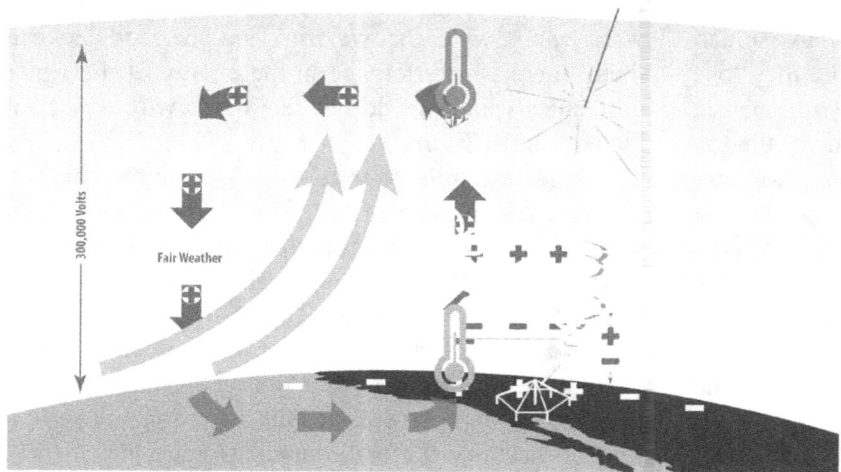

So that's why, in Asian countries, we see a lot of hot fountains—and probably also you have the special water systems in California—because water from fountains starts to evaporate, and it absorbs the heat and decreases the temperature in this area. That's why we create fountains: To decrease the temperature a little bit, where we have a hot climate.

And so, if we deal with ionization, we have the same effect. When the water condenses on ions, it releases heat. But if you decrease the condensation, you will decrease the temperature in this place. That's why it was discovered, the connection of the sharp decrease of galactic cosmic ray fluxes during the magnetic storms, with formation of the hurricanes.

Again, in Mexico, I have a good colleague, Jorge Pérez-Peraza, who is working on the connection of the fluxes of galactic cosmic rays and formation of hurricanes in the Atlantic and Pacific areas of Mexico. And he has very good statistics, that show that when you have a lot of Forbush decrease—so, an active Sun, many magnetic storms—this increases the probability of the formation of tropical cyclones and hurricanes.

And we published a paper showing the physical mechanisms: If you have a decrease of fluxes of galactic cosmic rays, you decrease the temperature on the level of the tropopause, and in such a way, you increase the temperature difference between the surface of the ocean and the tropopause. So, you sharply increase convection and help hurricanes to form, due to increased convection (**Figure 12**).

Galactic Cosmic Rays

Deniston: I think this is a remarkable thing you're saying, that these high-energy particles, not coming from our Earth, not coming from our star, but coming from all regions of interstellar space and the galaxy, are actually playing an active role in things like the strength of hurricanes or hurricane formation.

Pulinets: Yes, yes, yes. And there is—Israeli scientists Nir Shaviv and Ján Veizer discovered another effect of modulation of fluxes of galactic cosmic rays, with periods of Earth ice ages in the long-term history of our planet (**Figure 13a**). And they were able to demonstrate that it *could be*—this is hypothesis—could be connected with movement of the Solar System in the arms our spiral galaxy. And when the Solar System is inside the arms, that is, there is more dust, so there is less flux of the galactic cosmic rays. And between the arms, we have the larger fluxes of the galactic cosmic rays (**Figure 13b**). And these periods coincide, temporally, with periods of increased and decreased temperature of our planet.

Deniston: All these ionization effects, these cosmic radiation effects that you're describing here, they're constantly creating certain conditions in our atmosphere that affect how water vapor behaves, that affect

GALACTIC COSMIC RAY FLUX AND TEMPERATURE

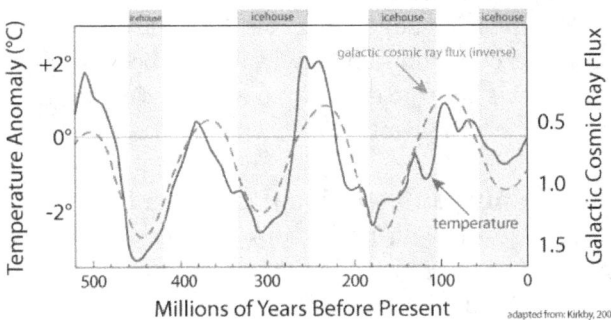

adapted from: Kirkby, 2008

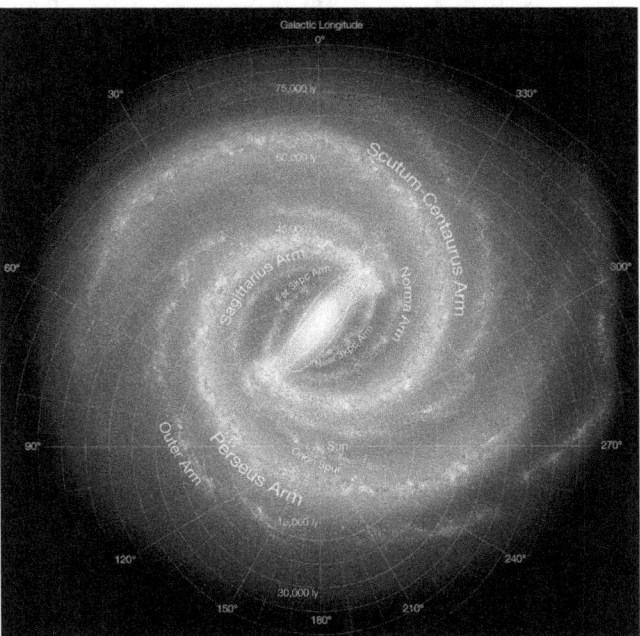

how weather behaves, that affect climate.

Pulinets: Yes, and we should not forget that with clouds, you have the shadows on the Earth. So the temperature variation is connected not only with the direct heat created by cosmic rays, but with the shadow: More clouds, more shadow; fewer clouds, you are open to the Sun. So these variations of temperature connected with shadow are also essential.

Deniston: Well, I just have to say, this kind of redefines what we mean when we think of the Earth's climate, because it's not—it's more like a solar and galactic climate than just an Earth climate.

Pulinets: We should take into account both of them. You see, you cannot say that it is only galactic. But the galaxy creates some contribution to the variations of climate.

Deniston: Mm-hmm. And so you're saying that this work being done with these ionization systems, is a way that we can begin to affect these types of parameters, create our own influence on these weather systems, the water cycle, and utilize that to our own benefit.

Pulinets: Yes, I think so. It is possible, but we should do it, very, very carefully. I suppose that there should be state or administrative control, because influencing the environment could be dangerous; you should have some limits, because you can create huge installations to make very large ionization, depending on the polarity; then you can increase the number of clouds, or decrease the number of clouds. Somebody will want to have a resort and have a lot of Sun; another one wants to produce grapes and have rains, and they could be neighbors, and then fight over whether you have clouds or don't have clouds! So these activities should be regulated, of course.

Responsible Water Management

Deniston: What would you think should be the next step for developing these systems, as you're saying, in

a mature and regulated way? Because I think this opens up a whole new potential, obviously for how mankind can deal with these challenges, like droughts, or like bad weather occurring that causes excess flooding.

This is a growing, major issue. Water is a huge issue, not just for the United States, but globally. There's many places in the world that are lacking fresh water, or they lack regular supplies. They get rain, then they get drought, and they get a little bit of rain again, and drought. It seems as if what you're defining here is an incredibly important perspective for how we could begin to, in a responsible, regulated way, we could begin to manage water in a completely new way, by managing how it operates in the atmosphere, not just how it operates once it lands on ground.

So, from your standpoint, what do you think would be the next steps to begin to develop this in a responsible manner?

Pulinets: I suppose we should organize open and clear, distinct experiments on this, with good scientific support, for scientists to be able to control and to see that such effects really exist. Because, let's say, traditional atmospheric scientists or meteorologists sometimes say it's not possible; so we should at least make these experiments, to demonstrate, first, to the scientific community, and second, to the public, that no danger exists. These effects are no more dangerous than a natural electric field.

I know that in some experiments in Mexico, the cows

came close to this installation, because they have a better feeling inside this electric field! So, this is a proof, that it is no danger to nature. And the birds feel these electric fields very well, so they do not approach them.

Deniston: And maybe also, you've been mostly discussing the activity that went on in Mexico. There are other companies in other places where these systems have been demonstrated, correct?

Pulinets: Yes. I know that such companies exist in Saudi Arabia, maybe in Australia; maybe some are already in Russia, but they are not doing active experiments. I know that there were experiments on ionization in Japan, over five years. But they were not connected with rain, they were connected with dispersing fogs in the mountain roads of Japan. So you create precipitation and decrease the fog, to improve the movement in tunnels and high mountains, where the fog forms very often.

Deniston: How long do you think it would take to get a demonstration system set up, say, maybe in the region somewhere in California, to demonstrate the validity of this technology?

Pulinets: Actually to put up the installation takes one to two weeks, and I suppose we need at least one year to check different seasons, to see Winter, Autumn, Spring, Summer, where we have the optimum conditions to create favorable conditions for this precipitation. And we should take into account also the farmers' planting calendar, to also meet their needs, and so on— not only for drinking, but for agriculture, basically.

But it seems to me, one year will be enough to set up experiments.

Deniston: Well, again, I think this is a very exciting and important perspective to be discussing, in this context of the drought in California, the water needs of other places in the world. Not only are there these technologies, but, as you're discussing, there is the theory behind these technologies which enable mankind to begin to address these problems in a new way.

Pulinets: We did not discuss this, in this presentation, because, OK, it should be presented in scientific conferences. I said, as a general thing, what happens. But the physics is not very complex, but at least you need to have some background, to understand these processes.

Deniston: And you've said that your work in studying earthquake precursors and how the lithosphere, and the atmosphere, and the ionosphere interact in the preparation process for earthquakes—the theoretical framework you've developed in studying that—has very valid applications for this weather control as well.

Pulinets: Yes, of course. It is the same physical process, and even the same environment, because the installation is near the ground. So we have only the different sources of ionization.

Maintaining International Cooperation

Deniston: Well, I think this is a very exciting and important perspective that we're discussing here. And I also think, just because we're speaking now from the United States to Russia, this is also an important area where we can have productive and healthy international collaboration between our countries.

Pulinets: Yes, and of course, in the conditions we have today, it may help us to improve our relationships, which have gone down a little bit during the last year. But our cooperation, for example, in space, in the International Space Station, and in physics, etc., never depended on any conditions, but was very firm, was very frank, and I suppose we should maintain these relationships.

Deniston: It certainly seems like a key area, because we're defining how mankind can address problems that are bigger than any one nation: You know, a drought's not just an issue for one part of the world, and not the other. These are the types of things that all mankind should be thinking about.

Pulinets: Yes, of course. It is a global problem, and all nations should unite to improve the condition.

Deniston: Do you have anything else to add in conclusion? I really appreciate your taking the time to go through some of the science and your background in this area. I think it's very important.

Pulinets: And I also want to thank you, for finding me and giving me the opportunity to explain how we can fight the droughts. We don't need too much money for these installations.

Deniston: It's relatively cheap to do. It's not an incredibly expensive operation.

Pulinets: For example, in comparison with the seeding from airplanes, this is moderately priced.

Deniston: Well, I thank you again for joining us, Professor Pulinets. It's always a pleasure to get a chance to speak to you and get your understanding of these things.

Pulinets: Thank you, Ben. And you are welcome to visit us.

Deniston: I would be very happy to. Thank you, and we'll have more on this very important subject on larouchepac.com. Thank you for joining us.

Albert Einstein's God

by Tony Papert

1. Prolog in Heaven

On a recent evening (May 5), the great American economist and philosopher Lyndon LaRouche discussed with some friends, including myself, the Galactic Principle which is the subject of this May 15 EIR. As that evening's discussion was coming to a close, Lyn said that because the Galaxy controls everything with which we are familiar, the Galaxy itself is the closest thing to the God which we must worship.

For me, that brought me back to an old preoccupation with the question of the nature of Albert Einstein's religion. Einstein had clearly been a totally pious man, who devoted his whole mind and his whole heart to the service of God all the time, as the Bible commands,— but, in his case, certainly not because the Bible commanded it.

At the same time, it was clear that Einstein had never worshipped the gods which are commonly worshipped in this country,—one of the crimes for which Socrates was executed. Einstein obviously did not worship the god of the Bumper-Sticker or the Lapel-Pin. He did not

Library of Congress

Albert Einstein

worship the god of "Let the markets solve it," nor the god of "Be practical,"—which are actually demons rather than gods.

Who or what did he worship?

2. Solvay, 1927 AD

Naive graduate students believe that the intense faction-fights at the 1927 Solvay Conference (basically, a huge, coordinated attack against Einstein), were occasioned by abstruse issues in so-called Quantum Mechanics. Nothing could be further from the truth. (Indeed, how peculiar that anyone would choose to dispute Quantum Mechanics with Einstein, after he had singlehandedly invented the whole field quite on his own, in the face of skepticism even from Max Planck.)

Rather, Solvay 1927 was the setting for the very deliberate, "FBI-style" mental-spiritual brutalization of Einstein,—no matter the pretextual issues.

Now, Niels the Terrible Bore was a mental case out of Denmark, who was a crony of the British Empire's arch-villain Bertrand Russell. It was this Bohr, who was the Kapo who tried to butcher Einstein mentally at Solvay,—just as Hitler was soon to do physically to millions of Europeans,—and not only to Einstein's fellow Jews. Einstein himself, simply outright refused to sell out,—he would, and did, die before doing that, after at least a lifetime's-worth of the most terrible coercive pressure. But, under the intense coercion, almost every one of Einstein's friends worldwide, publicly repudiated him sooner or later. Mostly sooner. Shades of "McCarthyism!"

But, among the real men and women of science at Solvay, several refused to denounce Einstein. (All the eunuchs did, of course.) Although Max Planck was implicitly a target of the same attack, this was apparently

The Empyrean, from illustrations of Dante's Divine Comedy by Gustave Doré.

never mentioned because of Planck's exalted status Erwin Schrödinger, the discoverer of wave mechanics was a prime target, but apparently refused to take the purge-trial seriously, in the belief that all his attackers were simply nuts,—which of course they were.

Indeed, a background in the history of the deadly faction-fights within the Socialist movement,—all fought out amidst the interventions of sundry police and intelligence agencies,—is a more important prerequisite for understanding the 1927 Solvay Conference than even the mathematics. The standard histories of the CPUSA, tell the story of a 1929 mission to Moscow by the leadership of that organization, then headed by Jay Lovestone. When their visit had been concluded, Lovestone and his friends found that they were somehow unable to leave Moscow. They could not get exit visas. They were trapped there, while Stalin picked them off one by one, and persuaded each of them to denounce Lovestone. At one point, he brought Lovestone and his few remaining holdouts to the Kremlin, to tell them, "When I'm done with you, only your wives will support you." And, indeed, once Stalin had made good on that threat, Lovestone was at last allowed to return to the USA,—where later he went to work for the FBI,—

that is, unless he had been working for the FBI all along.

The most hilarious apostasy of Solvay was that of Louis de Broglie, the young French genius whose fame was that he had discovered that every particle is simultaneously a wave. Maybe it should be noted here, that this discovery of de Broglie's was no mere morning mushroom, sprung out of the positivistic-like outlooks which are encouraged in science today. Rather, de Broglie, like Einstein, Planck, Kepler, and every other scientist who has ever made a really significant discovery, was a very close student of all of the history of science and philosophy,—and from original sources, not from textbooks. "Why do we believe this? When and where could we have gone wrong?" Any real scientist always asks himself these questions. The so-called "history of science," is not some separate field, to be mined by "historians of science," who are not scientists. It is always an integral part of science itself.

Now, de Broglie arguably owed his scientific renown to Einstein. De Broglie had hit on his particle-wave hypothesis as a young man in Paris. De Broglie's PhD examiner, the famous physicist Paul Langevin, had asked Einstein's advice before accepting his 1924 dissertation. Einstein not only read and supported the dissertation, but also communicated its importance to other physicists,—just the sort of thing he was doing constantly. If not for that, de Broglie might have remained unknown for years, or forever.

At Solvay 1927, Bohr's and some others' slashing attacks against Einstein, and Einstein's attempts to defend himself, were all conducted in hotel dining-rooms and other informal settings, away from the stuffy and boring public sessions of the Conference. It was in these eateries and the like, that Bohr and his crew, acting for Bertrand Russell, day after day hammered away, wore down and peeled off layer after layer of Einstein's support. De Broglie was also at these informal sessions,—*but* he understood only French, while everyone spoke exclusively in either English or German. Therefore, de Broglie could not follow any of these heated discussions (allegedly about quantum mechanics), which pitted Bohr and others against Einstein. But that did not stop him from announcing his defection from Einstein shortly after the conference ended.

From all the reports available to me, one could conclude that Einstein and Bohr, respectively, arrived at the conference roughly with equal numbers of supporters on both sides. The number of those who didn't know, or didn't care, was probably greater than either group,—and one remembers where Dante placed these sorts of people in his epic poem

Bohr left with greatly enhanced support, while Einstein left more or less as Jay Lovestone would leave Moscow. By the time Einstein had made it back to his home in Berlin, he was exhausted and subdued. But yet, the truth is still the truth if only one man believes it,—or if absolutely no one believes it,—as Einstein repeated precisely this watchword in myriad ways throughout his life. And no,—he had not abandoned the truth, nor would he ever.

3. Truth in Mathematics?

The obsession which maintains that the truths of science are to be found in mathematics, although it is axiomatic in the Boredom School of physics, is so evidently absurd that it is difficult to understand how any intelligent person could believe in it for half an hour. And looking at the question historically, no competent student doubts that Einstein had developed the General Relativity Theory years before he came upon the mathematics appropriate for General Relativity. Thus, provably, his discovery was not mathematical.

All that had been demanded of Einstein at Solvay, 1927 and later, was that he publicly repudiate causality, universality, order and the Good,—i.e., repudiate God. This is not to imply that causality+universality+order+ the Good was Einstein's God. Not at all. They are only predicates, and we know that Einstein's personal theology was a negative one like that of Nicholas of Cusa and other divines,—of a God absolutely above and beyond all predicates. (Although there is a lot more to it than just that.) *But,*—it is indisputable nonetheless, that anyone who repudiates causality, universality, order and the Good,—has repudiated God.

To replace Him, in this case, with a mental illness which claims that mere mathematical models dictate their terms to reality,—that is, dictate their terms to God. And now, having understood this much, you can now recognize Einstein's anguished protest against this insanity, in many of his most widely-quoted statements,—statements ostensibly about God. This is the mental illness which Schrödinger immediately recognized in those who were trying to persecute himself and Einstein. But the insoluble problem in explaining any of this to most audiences today, is that their education has precisely drilled-and-grilled them to repeat back, and perhaps even to believe, that mathematical models somehow secretly govern everything in the world,—as what Lyndon LaRouche once called, "the little green men underneath the floor-boards."

This is the conceit of the wildly-popular 1999 movie "Matrix," by the Wachowski siblings.[1]

4. Conclusion

Max Born was a weasel who sold out at the first opportunity, and at every opportunity. He spent forty years writing letters to Einstein, begging, pleading and threatening him to abandon his principles and join Born in his moral sewer. For forty years, Einstein declined. Einstein, for his part, tried to win Born back to truth and morality,—but to no avail.

The pretext which Born used was a correspondence between their two wives. Born's wife was a real piece of work,—always ready to snap up any new yoga, or other occultism,—or, for that matter, any new recipe. Max Born encouraged her to share all of these fads with Einstein's wife (assuming that she needed any encouragement). And, because the letter from one wife to the other wife would cost the same postage-stamp anyway, the husbands would usually write their own letter and stick it into the same envelope.

In the end, it was Max Born who published this correspondence as a book. Why would he do this, since the correspondence simply demonstrates his, Born's absolute failure to make any progress towards his goal of corrupting Einstein? My conclusion is that he published the letters simply to show how hard he had tried. To show his masters,—Bertrand Russell probably the most important of them,—all the effort which Born had expended on

---

1. The art of the Wachowskis, is artificial induction of psychosis. For more on this, see Louis A. Sass, *Madness and Modernism*, Basic Books, 1992.

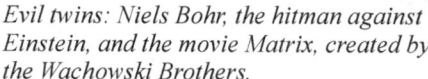

Evil twins: Niels Bohr, the hitman against Einstein, and the movie Matrix, created by the Wachowski Brothers.

intellectual fire burned out his physical resources prematurely. Einstein always looked older than he actually was. More than once in his life he was desperately ill, but always with an apparently good chance of recovery. But in 1954 the rapid decline of his physical forces became alarmingly manifest. When, on April 15, 1955, he was transferred to the hospital of Princeton, he knew that no hope was left. In the morning of April 18 his life ended. He died with the same simplicity and humility with which he lived. Calmly and unperturbed, with no pathos, no sentimentality, no regret, he waited for the approaching death. 'Even in his death he showed us how to live,' were the words of his daughter Margot. 'Homo liber de nulla re minus quam de morte cogitat,' said the great Dutch philosopher Spinoza, whom Einstein held in particularly high esteem. 'The free man thinks of nothing less than of death.' Albert Einstein was a free man."

Are we now any closer to the answer to our question about the God of Albert Einstein? I think we are closer. I think we have come to glimpse the reality that God is only to be found where Einstein sought to find Him, in his mission, in his journey through the unitary combination of art, science, morality, and his sort of religion, all seen as one single Truth. No easy task, you reply? Perhaps not, "But," as Spinoza concluded his *Ethics* in 1675, "all noble things are as difficult as they are rare."

their behalf,—even if in the end it achieved nothing.

Einstein was offered refuge in the United States, at Princeton University's Institute for Advanced Study. But the conditions offered to him were so restrictive, that he considered them equivalent to "prison." Einstein sought to renegotiate his contract, and succeeded in increasing his freedom to some extent.

At Princeton, Einstein was almost shunned for his unfashionable views, and actually took little part in scientific discourse in the United States, as amazing as that may sound. Among other wry remarks, he said, "The Jews consider me a saint. The Americans consider me a museum-piece. My colleagues consider me a mountebank."

Einstein's great joy at Princeton, was his daily walks with Kurt Gödel, the Austrian scientist who had publicly shattered Bertrand Russell's reputation by proving that Russell's fantasy of the axiomatization of arithmetic, in his *Principia Mathematica*, was impossible. If Einstein was "almost shunned" in the United States, then Gödel was actually shunned, as were his friends. The psychological quirks which some have gleefully discovered in Gödel, if there is any truth at all to those reports, may have stemmed from the severe persecution and punishment he suffered here.

Einstein's friend, Cornelius Lanczos, reports his death as follows. "As the years passed by, the raging

Further Reading:

Manjit Kumar, *Quantum*, W.W. Norton, 2011.—This is the best book I've found on what actually went on at Solvay, 1927.

Cornelius Lanczos, *The Einstein Decade*, Elek Science, London, 1974.—This precious book by a lifelong friend of Einstein, is full of material unavailable elsewhere. For only one example: Lanczos summarizes in English, every one of Einstein's numerous contributions to *Annalen der Physik* for 1905-15.

Einstein on Kepler

Albert Einstein wrote this article on the 300th anniversary of Kepler's death, for the Frankfurter Zeitung, *Nov. 9, 1930. It was translated by* EIR.

Precisely in such a troubled and turbulent time as ours, when it is hard to summon up joy about mankind and the progress of human affairs, it is especially comforting to think of such a great and serene person as Kepler.

He lived at a time when the very conception of universal lawfulness of nature was not at all established. How great must have been his faith in such lawfulness, to have the strength to endure decades of patient, difficult work—supported by no one and understood by few—in the empirical investigation of planetary movement and its lawful mathematical expression! If we want to commemorate him appropriately, we have to look as closely as possible at his problem and the stages of its solution.

Copernicus had opened the eyes of the best thinkers to the idea that the apparent motions of the planets could most clearly be understood as orbits around the Sun, which itself is conceived as stationary. If a planet simply moved in a circle with the Sun at the center, it would have been conceptually simple to discover how such motions would look from the Earth. But much more complex phenomena were involved, so the task was far more difficult. So to begin with, these motions had to be investigated empirically, using Tycho Brahe's observations of the planets. Only then could one think, for the first time, of discovering the universal laws that govern these motions.

To imagine how difficult it was even to determine the actual orbital motions, consider the following: One never sees where a planet is actually located, but only in what direction it is visible at any given time from the Earth, which, however, is itself moving in an unknown way around the Sun. The difficulties seem all but insurmountable.

Kepler had to find a way to bring order out of this chaos. First of all, he realized that he would have to try to determine the movement of the Earth itself. This would have been simply impossible, had only the Sun, the Earth, and the fixed stars existed, but no other planets. It would be impossible to establish anything empirically, except how the line from Sun to Earth changes during the course of the year (the apparent motion of the Sun against the fixed stars). It could be ascertained that these directions of the Sun-Earth line all lay in a constant plane with respect to the fixed stars, at least to the degree of observational accuracy that existed then, without telescopes. It could also be determined how the Sun-Earth line rotates around the Sun. It could thus be observed that the angular velocity of this motion changes in a regular way, during a year. But this would not help much, it would still not be known how much the distance between the Sun and Earth changes in a year. Only when the changes in this distance in a year were known, could the true shape of the Earth's orbit be discovered, as well as how this pathway is traversed.

IoANNIS KEPPLERI
Mathematici Cæsarei
hanc Imaginem

Frankfurt University

Johannes Kepler

The Lantern of Mars

Kepler found a marvelous way out of this dilemma. First of all, observations of the Sun showed that its apparent path across the background of the fixed stars sped up at certain times of year, but that the angular velocity of this motion was the same at the same point in the astronomical year—i.e., that the rotational speed of the Earth-Sun line was the same at each time of year, when seen against the same location among the fixed stars. It could therefore be surmised that the Earth's orbit was a *closed* curve, with the Earth returning every year to the same place, in the same way. That was by no means self-evident, *a priori*. For the advocate of the Copernican system, it was almost certain that this must also apply to the paths of the other planets.

That certainly made things easier. But how could the true shape of the Earth's orbit be determined? Think of a brightly shining lantern **M**, somewhere in the plane of the Earth's orbit; its position remains constant, so that it defines a fixed point of triangulation from which to construct the path of the Earth's orbit, a point which the Earth's inhabitants can take a sighting of, at any time of year. This lantern **M** is further from the Sun than the Earth is. Such a lantern helped to define the Earth's orbit, as follows:

First of all, every year there is a time at which the Earth E is aligned with both the Sun **S** and the lantern **M**. At that time, take a sighting from the Earth **E** toward the lantern **M**, right along the line **SM** (Sun-lantern). Imagine that the latter [the lantern—ed.] is affixed to the vault of the heavens. Now imagine the Earth being in a different place, at a different time. One would be able to see both the Sun **S** and the lantern **M**, from the Earth, forming the triangle **SEM**, with the angle at E being known. But also, from direct observation of the Sun, one can determine the direction of **SE** against the fixed stars, while previously the direction of line **SM** had been calculated against the fixed stars. But in the triangle **SEM**, we also know the angle at S. Thus we can construct on a piece of paper an arbitrary baseline **SM**, and with both the angles at **E** and at **S** known, we can also construct triangle **SEM**. This construction could be carried out frequently during the year, each time plotting on the paper the Earth's position **E**, with the relevant time/date for its position with respect to the constant baseline **SM**. The Earth's orbit could be empirically calculated in this way—except, of course, for its absolute size.

But, you will ask, where did Kepler get the lantern **M**? His own genius and Nature's beneficence (in this case) gave it to him. The planet Mars provided an example, and the length of the Martian year was known—i.e., one revolution of Mars around the Sun. The Sun, Earth, and Mars might one day line up exactly in a straight line. This location of Mars recurs after one, two, etc. Martian years, since Mars also moves in a closed orbit. At these known moments, **SM** therefore provides the same baseline, while the Earth is always somewhere else in its orbit. Observations of the Sun and Mars at these exact moments thus provide a way to determine the true orbit of the Earth, in which, at each point, Mars plays the role of the imaginary lantern described above! That is how Kepler was able to find the true shape of the Earth's orbit, and how it is traversed by the Earth, such that we subsequent generations of people—Europeans, Germans, or even Swabians[1]—could marvel and praise him.

From the Imagined, to the Observed

Now comes the second, and no less difficult, part of Kepler's life's work. The orbits were empirically established, but their laws still had to be figured out from the empirical evidence. First, to pose a conjecture about the mathematical form of the orbital curve; and then, to check it with a phenomenal amount of numerical data. If it doesn't work, then come up with another hypothesis and work through checking that one. After a prodigious search, he got it: The orbit is an ellipse; the Sun is located at one focus. He also discovered the law governing the rate of change of the speed of revolution: that the Sun-planet line sweeps through equal areas in equal times. Finally, he also discovered, that the square of the orbital period is equal to the cube of the ellipse's major axis.

Our admiration for this wonderful man is joined with another feeling of admiration and veneration, not for any person, but for the mysterious harmony of Nature into which we were born. In ancient times, men already thought about lines of the simplest conceivable regularity. Among these, the foremost, next to the straight line and the circle, was the ellipse (and also the hyperbola). We see these latter forms realized, at least in close approximation, in the orbits of the heavenly bodies.

It seems that human reason first has to independently construct the forms, before we can detect them in things. Kepler's marvelous life's work shows us especially beautifully, that cognition cannot blossom from sheer empirics, but from the comparison of what is imagined, with what is observed.

---

1. Both Kepler and Einstein were Swabians—ed.

The First Solvay: 350 BC Aristotle's Assault on Plato

by Susan J. Kokinda

May 11—If one looks at the principles embedded in Plato's scientific masterwork, *Timaeus*, especially from the vantage point of the work of Einstein and Vernadsky in the Twentieth Century, one can understand why the oligarchy had to carry out a brutal assault on Plato and his Academy, an assault led by Aristotle, which ultimately resulted in the imposition of Euclid's mind-deadening geometry on the world, and the millennia-long set-back of Western civilization.

That the oligarchical enemy of mankind responds with brute force to those philosophers and scientists, who act on the basis of human creativity, was captured in the opening of Aeschylus' great tragedy, "Prometheus Bound." On orders from Zeus, the Olympian ruler, Kratos (might) and Bios (force) oversaw Prometheus' punishment. In the opening scene, Kratos and Bios force Prometheus' fellow god, Hephaestus to impale him with nails and chain him to a mountainside, in retribution for the crime of imparting to mankind the knowledge of fire, astronomy, agriculture, and the other arts and sciences which distinguish man from beast.

From Philolaus to Kepler

Plato's great dialogue on ontology, the *Timaeus*, presents a universe which can be known by man, because man, like the universe, is ensouled and noëtic. Space is not empty, but rather a function of physical space, which Plato struggles to communicate using a "bastard" concept. Time is not a yardstick outside of the universe, but rather a moving image of eternity. Man cannot know this universe through his senses. But, through his mind, he can discover the principles of the universe by examining the shadows cast by the geometry of the Platonic solids and the harmonies of music. It is a living universe, created by a single God who created it to be good, and God was happy in its creation.

Lurking in the shadows of the future, one sees Einstein's relativity, Planck's quantum. and Vernadsky's noösphere. But in the immediate foreground was Philolaus of Croton (in Italy), the earliest Pythagorean from whom any fragments survive. (Fortunately, Philolaus himself survived the arson-murder of most of the second generation of Pythagoreans in Croton, and relocated to Greece.) In the footprints of those fragments walks the *Timaeus*.

Philolaus' fragments are like a prelude to the investigations which fill the *Timaeus*. And so, astronomy, geometry, and harmony were at the core of the work of Plato's Academy. Indeed, every member was given the assignment of developing an hypothesis to account for the motions of the heavenly bodies.

And it is to Philolaus that Johannes Kepler refers, in his denunciation of Aristotle's *On the Heavens*.[1] Referring to Philolaus' assertion that the earth travels around a central fire, Kepler said "They [the Pythagoreans] spoke in a veiled way, by fire they understood the Sun, and I agree with them, that the Sun is in the center of the world and never moves away from this place, and that on the other hand, the Earth moves once in one year around the Sun, … as otherwise also five other wandering stars (the planets), with this order.…"

We will hear Kepler speak again on the subject of Aristotle.

It's NOT Academic

One of the greatest ironies embedded in the modern use (or, perhaps, perversion) of a word, is the concept of "academic." Plato's Academy, from whence the word comes, was anything but "academic."[2] Nothing could

---

1. First translated into English in *21st Century Science & Technology*, George Gregory, translator, <u>Winter 2001-2002</u>
2. Indeed, the funds that Plato used to found the Academy in 388 BC were ultimately unneeded ransom funds that had been raised to save Plato from being sold into slavery by the Syracusan tyrant Dionysius I.

A mosaic of Plato's academy, found in Pompeii.

capture this more poignantly than the mortal wounding of Theaetetus, the great geometer and member of the Academy, in a battle against Persia's allies in 369 BC.

Never forget that Plato's thinking was shaped, not only by the life of Socrates, but also by his death at the hands of the Athenian *democracy* in 399 BC. One can relive the impact on Plato of both that life and death, in the extraordinary *Phaedo* dialogue, where he describes Socrates' final hours, as Socrates engages in an extraordinary dialogue on the immortality of the human soul with two of Philolaus' students, Cebes and Simmias.

And so, from Socrates' death until his own in 348 BC, Plato and his forces led a strategic, political, and most important, intellectual battle against the Zeusian oligarchy.

After the death of Socrates, Plato left Athens for twelve years, on a scientific and strategic mission. After visiting Megara, he traveled to Egypt, the wellspring of ancient scientific and astronomical knowledge, as Plato identifies it in the *Timaeus* through the person of Solon. Egypt was also a key ally in the fight against Persia. From Egypt, Plato traveled to Sicily, to embark on the first of three attempts to develop a "philosopher king," or at least a competent ally within the ruling family of Syracuse. His "Italian project" was coordinated with the third-generation Pythagorean, Archytas of Tarentum, who, at Plato's request, provided him the works of Philolaus.

From his return from Syracuse and the founding of

the Academy in 388 BC, until his death in 348 BC, and in fact, beyond his death, Plato created a scientific and political force which threatened the very existence of the Persian (better, Babylonian/Persian) Empire.

On the strategic front, his allies in Greece and Egypt engaged the Persians, or their satraps and allies directly in battle. In 356 BC, Plato's Phocian allies seized the Temple of Delphi, from which the oligarchy manipulated leaders and the public alike through its oracles, and into which Greek city-states deposited their treasuries. Delphi was like the Federal Reserve and the mass media all rolled up into one, so its capture and control by the Phocians was a crippling blow. The short-lived success of Plato's ally Dion in defeating Dionysius II in 357 BC, temporarily put Syracuse into friendly hands.

Enter Aristotle

But most of these victories were holding actions, which ultimately did not last. The real danger, as Zeus understood when he chained Prometheus to the mountainside, was the concept of man as it was developed in the Academy. The proliferation of that power was (and is) ultimately more deadly to oligarchism than military conquest.

As embedded in all of Plato's dialogues, but never so powerfully stated as by the soon-to-be-executed Socrates in the *Phaedo*,—that which makes man immortal is his ability to free himself from the sense-certainties of the body, thereby allowing the mind to discover universal principles. In the conclusion of the *Phaedo*, Socrates chides some of his companions for bewailing his coming death. They, unlike Cebes and Simmias, never seem to grasp the point of the discussion: Socrates is not his mortal body,—he is his mind and his soul, and will not die.

Think of the challenge of this idea to the Imperial systems of the ancient world, based on slavery and the degradation of man to the image of an animal. Think of the threat posed by Plato's *Meno* dialogue, in which Socrates causes a *slave boy* to discover how to double a square, and to thereby discover a power of his own mind.

And, as made clear in the *Timaeus*, that power of mind gives man a grasp of the non-sensual processes which govern the universe, and, in doing so, allows him to act effectively on the world. And with that, Plato made mincemeat of his philosophical opponents throughout his dialogues. Whether it was the sterility of the Eleatic School of Parmenides, or the Nietzschean thuggery of Callicles in the *Gorgias* dialogue, Plato mowed down the ideologies which kept people in a state of mental, if not physical, slavery.

The oligarchy could not tolerate Plato's breakthroughs. Aristotle, the son of a Macedonian court doctor and functionary, was brought into play and dispatched to Athens in 368 BC, while Plato and Xenocrates (a future head of the Academy and a major figure in later battles) were on a second mission to Syracuse to attempt to recruit the son of Dionysius. (They failed.) Aristotle had first passed through the school of Isocrates to get his mission specs. Isocrates, a member of a rich family who had fallen on difficult financial times, founded the first actual "school" of rhetoric. Prior to that, Greece had been beset by traveling sophists, who wandered from city to city, training the children of rich Athenians in the art of convincing people, or lying "prettily." But it was time to establish a command center, out of which to deploy enemy operations. Isocrates himself would later become the conduit for the idea of splitting up the Persian Empire, into a more manageable Eastern Division, as against a Western Division which was to be ruled by Philip of Macedon. We will see how that turned out below.

For the next two decades, Aristotle "bored from within." The oligarchs' problem was how replace Plato with anti-human nonsense, while maintaining the pretense of preserving his teaching. One of the more ridiculous arguments of so-called scholars, especially of the Leo Strauss school, is that Plato had "hidden teachings." How do we know there were such teachings? Because Aristotle's description, in his own writings, of Plato's ideas is so different from Plato's, that it must represent the "hidden teachings" of the Academy! One modern author, Harold Cherniss, had the good sense to point out that Aristotle either didn't understand Plato, or misrepresented him.

That is putting it too mildly. Aristotle was deployed to destroy Plato.

The ancient historian Aelian decribes the following, which took place around 350 BC:

> Once when Xenocrates went off on a visit to his homeland (Chalcedon), Aristotle set upon Plato, surrounding himself with a gang of his own partisans, including Mnason of Phocis and people

From the 'Timaeus'

Let us now state the Cause wherefor he that constructed it, constructed Becoming and the All. He was good, and in him that is good no envy ariseth ever concerning anything; and being devoid of envy He desired that all should be, so far as possible, like unto Himself. This principle, then, we shall be wholly right in accepting from men of wisdom as being above all the supreme originating principle of Becoming and the Cosmos. For God desired that, so far as possible, all things should be good and nothing evil; wherefore, when He took over all that was visible, seeing that it was not in a state of rest but in a state of discordant and disorderly motion, He brought it into order out of disorder, deeming that the former state is in all ways better than the latter. For Him who is most good, it neither was nor is permissible to perform any action save what is most fair. As He reflected, therefore, He perceived that of such creatures as are by nature visible, none that is irrational will be fairer, comparing wholes with wholes, than the rational; and further, that reason cannot possibly belong to any apart from Soul. So because of this reflexion He constructed reason within soul and soul with body as He fashioned the All, that so the work He was executing might be of its nature most fair and most good. Thus, then, in accordance with the likely account, we must declare that this Cosmos has verily come into existence as a Living Creature (Being) endowed with soul and reason owing to the providence of God.

—*Timaeus*, Loeb Edition, R.G. Bury translation, 29E

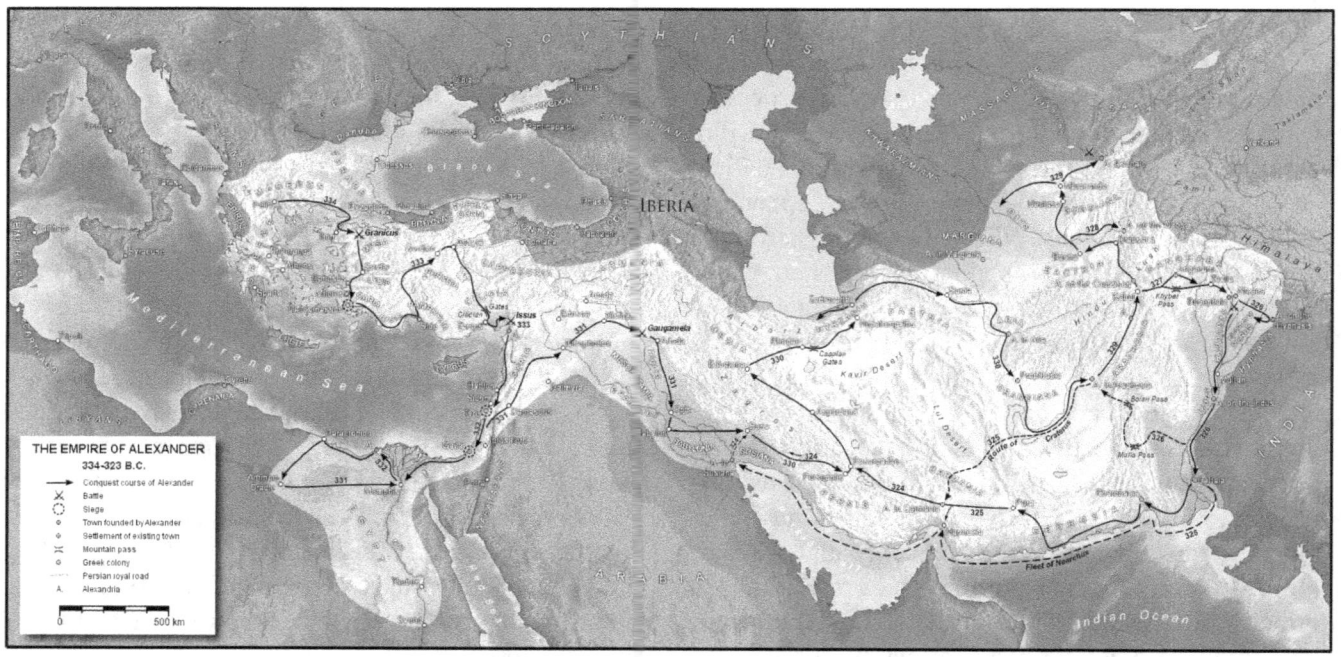

THE EMPIRE OF ALEXANDER
334–323 B.C.
→ Conquest course of Alexander
✕ Battle
◯ Siege
○ Town founded by Alexander
◇ Settlement of existing town
✕ Mountain pass
○ Greek colony
···· Persian royal road
A. Alexandria
0   500 km

like that. Speusippus at that time was ill, and for this reason was unable to stand by Plato. Plato was by now eighty years of age, and at the same time, because of his age, was to some extent losing his memory. So Aristotle devised a plot and set an ambush for him, and began to put questions to him very aggressively and in a way 'elenctically,' and was plainly behaving unjustly and unfeelingly. For this reason, Plato left the concourse outside, and walked about inside with his companions. (Cited in Aelian, *Varia Historia* 3.19)

Aelian reports that Xenocrates returned and rallied the pro-Plato forces, returned Plato to his position, and scolded Speusippus for failing to defend Plato.

Aristotle's boldness had undoubtedly been bolstered by the ascension of Philip of Macedon to the throne in 359 BC, since Philip and those who sponsored him, had been the patrons of Aristotle's family. In the years between Philip's taking power and Aristotle's at-

Alexander the Great

tempted 350 BC coup at the Academy, the battle between the oligarchical forces and Plato's networks had been intense, with the tactical situation shifting back and forth. The year 353 BC saw the defeat of some of Plato's allies. Philip defeated the Phocians, thus re-establishing Delphi, and Dion was assassinated, ending his short-lived rule in Syracuse.

Thus, from this position of growing strength, Aristotle rode out the failed Academy coup, and waited for Plato's death in 348 BC. At that point, Aristotle left the Academy to launch the attack from the outside,—an attack which, a generation later, resulted in the creation of Euclid's *Elements* (and possibly the creation of "Euclid" himself, since absolutely nothing is known of his life).

Alexander versus Aristotle

With the death of Plato in 348 BC, Aristotle left the Academy to go on permanent diplomatic assignment for Philip, often accompanied by his nephew Callisthenes. In 346 BC, Isocrates, Aristotle's real teacher, penned the "Isocrates Plan" urging Philip to take over from the now-incompetent Persians, as ruler of the "Western Division" of the Empire.

But while Aristotle was running around doing Philip's dirty work, Plato's networks had another plan,—recruit Philip's son, Alexander. *Indeed, one of the most enduring lies of history, is the claim that Alexander the Great was tutored by Aristotle.[3] The truth is that Alexander the Great was an intellectual project of Plato's Academy,—in particular, of the very Xenocrates who had defended Plato from Aristotle in 350 BC.* In the list of the titles of Xenocrates' works (of which not one fragment exists) are four books dedicated to Alexander,

---

3. As historian A.H. Chroust writes in his exhaustive work on Aristotle, there are no contemporary claims that Aristotle tutored Alexander. This rewriting of history emerged several centuries later.

and written at his request. Other members of the Academy traveled to Macedon to tutor Alexander directly. Alexander's reign from 336 BC, when he took over from Philip, whom he probably had killed, to 323 BC, fell entirely within Xenocrates' leadership of the Academy (339 to 314 BC).

Not only was Alexander not a student of Aristotle, *he was almost poisoned by Aristotle's nephew, Callisthenes, whom Aristotle had placed in Alexander's retinue. Alexander executed Callisthenes in 327 BC.*

In the thirteen years of his rule, Alexander crushed Persian rule, from Egypt, through Greece and Asia Minor, to Persia itself, and beyond to India. Isocrates' plan had failed. There was no Eastern and Western Division of the Persian Empire, because there was no Persian Empire. Instead, a student of Plato's heirs had conquered much of the known world.

From Aristotle

Perceptions are always true; it is intellect that introduces errors. *De Anima*

Since, according to common agreement, there is nothing outside and separate in existence from sensible spatial magnitudes, the objects of thought are all in sensible forms, both abstract objects and all the states and affections of sensible things. Hence, no one can learn or understand anything in the absence of senses, and when the mind is actively aware of anything, it is necessarily aware of it along with an image, for images are like sensuous contents....

While in respect of all the other senses we fall below many species of animals, in respect to touch we far excel all other species in exactness of discrimination. That is why man is the most intelligent of all animals. *De Anima*

Aristotle

The whole subject of moral virtue and of statecraft is bound up with the question of pleasures and pains; for if a man employs these well he will be good, if badly bad.... We have now sufficiently shown that moral virtue consists in observance of a mean ... of holding a middle position between two vices.... As it is hard to hit the exact mean, we ought to choose the lesser of the two evils."

Nicomachean Ethics

The slave is a living possession and property ... an instrument. The master is only the master of the slave: He does not belong to him, whereas the slave is not only the slave of his master, but wholly belongs to him.... For that some should rule and others be ruled, is a thing not only necessary, but expedient. From the hour of their birth, some are marked out for subjugation, others for rule.

Politics

But, where Callisthenes had failed, another Aristotle partisan succeeded. One of Philip's chief operatives had been Antipater, whom Philip had made governor of Macedon, and whom Alexander later made governor of Macedon and Greece. Alexander should have known better. Antipater was so close to Aristotle that he was made the executor of Aristotle's will. By 324 BC, Alexander began to suspect Antipater and dispatched troops back to Athens to bring him back to Alexander's camp, probably to execute him. Instead, Antipater sent his son, Cassander, who succeeded in poisoning Alexander in 323 BC. Aristotle could die a happy man in 322 BC.

The Real Coup

But the Imperial oligarchs could not be secure in their success. Plato was dead, Alexander assassinated. Yet, in the words of Socrates in the *Phaedo*, they were not dead. Plato's ideas could yet again give rise to another Alexander. Worse, they might become the basis for developing a population which would not tolerate oligarchical rule, of whatever geographical persuasion. The spread of Aristotle's "ideas" had to be reinforced.

Cassander returned to Greece, after killing Alexander, and appointed one of Xenocrates' political enemies, Demetrius of Phaleron, to rule Athens. In the political turmoil of the post-Alexander era, Demetrius eventually fled Athens in 307 BC, and arrived in Alexandria, Egypt, where he was appointed the head of the Library at Alexandria.

Demetrius of Phaleron, the appointee of that Cassander who was the son of the executor of Aristotle's will and who then killed Alexander, brought Euclid to the Library. Aristotle's assault on Plato's Academy had reached its culmination. Did Euclid even exist? Who knows? But whichever of Aristotle's intellectual heirs put together Euclid's *Elements*, they carried out a monstrous fraud. The geometrical work of Plato's Academy, as well as other work, was gathered together in one place and beaten to death. Euclid reduced the geometrical concepts of the Academy, which were understood to be the shadows of physical processes, to mere formulas and constructs built upon the assumptions of linear space as observed by the senses.

Some centuries later, in his *Commentaries on the First Book of Euclid's Elements*, the neo-Platonist Proclus spilled the beans on Euclid, and identified which of the Platonic and Pythagorean geometers and scientists had made the actual breakthroughs, which were then beaten to death by Euclid. Among them were Archytas, Theaetetus, Eudoxus, Menaechmus, and Theodius and Athenaeus. The latter two lived at the Academy and made their own arrangement of the *Elements of Geometry*. Proclus' book is not so much a commentary on Euclid, as it is an attempt to re-establish a Platonic understanding of geometry.

Out of the Darkness

In his first book, the *Mysterium Cosmographicum*, Johannes Kepler acknowledged exactly what Proclus had done. In a passage cited by Kepler, Proclus says:

> …next, we must ascertain what being can fittingly be ascribed to mathematical genera and species. Should we admit that they are derived from sense objects, either by abstraction as is commonly said, or by collection of particulars to one common definition? Or should we rather assign them to an existence prior to sense objects, as Plato demands…? … *And if we say that the soul produces them by having their patterns in her own essence, and that these offspring are projections of forms previously existing in her, we shall be in agreement with Plato and shall have found the truth with regard to mathematical being (emphasis added).*

Kepler continues:

> Proclus Diadochus, in the four books which he published on the First Book of Euclid, explicitly played the part of the theoretical philosopher dealing with a mathematical subject. If he had left to us commentaries on the Tenth Book of Euclid as well, he would both have freed our geometers from ignorance, if he had not been neglected, and relieved me totally from this toil of explaining and distinguishing features of geometrical objects. For from the very outset, it is readily apparent that those distinctions between *entities of the mind* would have been known, since he established the basic principles of the whole essence of mathematics, as the same which also pervade all entities and generate them all from themselves, that is to say the end

and the endless, or the limit and the unlimited, recognizing the limit or boundary as the form, the unlimited as the matter of geometrical objects (emphasis added).

The doctrines of Aristotle and Euclid, to which billions of minds have been subjected, whether in the form of direct indoctrination, or in the form of subjugation to a system created by such ideas, can only be imposed by the forceful elimination of the minds and ideas which stand in opposition to them.

Return again to Kepler's attack on Aristotle's *On the Heavens.* Kepler explains that the breakthroughs of the Pythagoreans, and implicitly the Platonic Academy, were obscured because of persecution, and

...on account of the reputation of Aristotle who rejected this teaching (although he did not yet fully understand it), this teaching was suppressed, and particularly because it was difficult to understand, it was nearly forgotten over the time of 1800 years; and finally there were no more Pythagorean philosophers, among whom alone this teaching was to be found.

One can lament that the last century was lost to a scientific Dark Age and the ensuing wars and destruction of lives and minds, resulting from the attacks on Einstein and Planck. This is particularly painful because we are living it. But imagine where mankind would be, were it not for the nearly two millennia lost between Plato's *Timaeus* and Kepler. Mankind would not be just discovering the galactic principle,—we would be living it.

Plato's Seventh Letter

Plato, in the great, autobiographical Seventh Letter, written after the death of his friend Dion, ridiculed the assertion by Dionysius II that he had written a book about Plato's philosophy.

There does not exist, nor will there ever exist, any treatise of mine dealing therewith. For it does not at all admit of verbal expression like other studies, but, as a result of continued application to the subject itself and communion therewith, it is brought to birth in the soul on a sudden, as a light that is kindled by a leaping spark, and thereafter it nourishes itself. *341C*

Plato puts the reader through an exercise in the discovery of the idea, not the form, of the circle, and then concludes:

Vatican Museum

Plato

For in learning these objects it is necessary to learn at the same time both what is false and what is true of the whole of Existence, and that through the most diligent and prolonged investigation; ... and it is by means of the examination of each of these objects, comparing one with another—names and definitions, visions and sense perceptions—proving them by kindly proofs and employing questionings and answerings that are void of envy—it is by such means, and hardly so, that there bursts out the light of intelligence and reason (nous) regarding each object in the mind of him who uses every effort of which mankind is capable. *344B*

For the writings of Dionysius were not meant as aids to memory, since *there is no fear lest anyone should forget the truth if once he grasps it with his soul, seeing that it occupies the smallest possible space* (emphasis added). *344*

Sputnik Interviews LaRouche on V-E Day

May 9—*On May 7, Russia's Sputnik News Agency interviewed World War II veteran Lyndon LaRouche about Victory in Europe Day, celebrating the Allies military defeat of fascism in the European theater. Below is the written exchange.*

Sputnik: Moscow is holding a Victory Day parade on May 9, and amid the current tensions between the West and Russia, a lot of world leaders will not attend the events. What do you think about that?

LaRouche: I think the Victory Parade should be considered as necessary.

Lyndon H. LaRouche, Jr.

LPAC-TV

Sputnik: Do you think that the role of the Soviet Army in the victory over Nazi Germany has recently been underestimated? Why do you think this is happening?

LaRouche: The Soviet Army's role in the combat against a Nazi regime at that time had been historically essential.

Sputnik: Do you think that young people in the West know the history, including World War II events, well? And why?

LaRouche: In the main, the generally post-adolescent and adult population of the Transatlantic powers of today, have virtually little to no comprehension of the meaning of human life—in that region, in particular. It is most notable, as for the cases of Europe and North America, that the quality of moral and related human life of persons among those nations, has been in a prevailing moral degeneration since the year 1900, as such of that time as the satanically evil, British monster, Bertrand Russell. The rate of such de-

generation has tended to be accelerated, not only from the span since 1900, but with an increasing relative influence, downward, up to the present date.

Sputnik: How do you think the role of the Soviet Army is presented nowadays?

LaRouche: With the effects of the attempted assassination of U.S. President Reagan, the general direction of U.S. national cultural life, has been one of an accelerating rate of political, moral, and scientific degeneration of accelerated economic and moral decline of North America and Central Europe, all promoted, essentially, by the increased self-degradation of the economies (per capita), and the declining morality of the leading powers of the Northerly regions of the Transatlantic zone. That process of decline has been continued, there, from its beginning, in the year 1900 A.D. of David Hilbert and of Bertrand Russell, until the present. Otherwise, the role of the Soviet defense of civilization during the so-called World War II period, still remains a crucial element of a struggle for all mankind.

Sputnik: Do you think that the far-right and neo-Nazi groups are growing and becoming more widespread? Why do you think this is happening?

LaRouche: The old Nazis, and the old British Empire, remain still the chief force of global evils presently. It is threatened to be much worse; it is that simple.

Sputnik: And/or anything else you could share with us on that, please?

LaRouche: Is there hope, despite all this? Yes. That prospect requires no further word, but, to the wise, only a suggestion of the meaning of what I have said here.